Rib Eye Shabu-Shabu, page 57

The
Asian
Hot Pot
COOKBOOK

Family-friendly One Pot Meals

AMY KIMOTO-KAHN

TUTTLE Publishing

Tokyo | Rutland, Vermont | Singapore

Contents

Pork Sukiyaki, page 70

Broths. Bases. Sauces & More

Chicken Hot Pots

Beef Hot Pots

Pork Hot Pots

Chanko Nabe Sumo Hot Pot, page 44

Vietnamese Oxtail Hot Pot, page 112

Why I Wrote This Book

I'm a *yonsei* — a fourth-generation Japanese-American. My parents were both born in California. My mom, Yvonne, is from San Francisco, and my father, Hayato, is from Los Angeles. In 1941, just two months after the Japanese bombing of Pearl Harbor, all people of Japanese ancestry in the United States were forced into internment camps. Two-thirds of the more than 120,000 people who were interned were American-born citizens, just like my parents. Both my parents and their families were given ten days to pack up only what they could carry and leave their homes.

During my parents' time in college, there was still postwar prejudice, and they were excluded from joining social groups, such as sororities and fraternities. It was at the University of Southern California that my mom decided to form her own group with her female Japanese-American friends, and thus The Dames came to be. They were the Martha Stewarts of their time. They married, had children and hosted elaborate gourmet evenings with menus including both Japanese and American dishes. The parties were hosted at different homes and the theme changed for each party. I have such clear memories of helping set the table with fine china and silver, assisting Mom at the kitchen counter and giving a helping hand with the dishes. It was an initiation of sorts.

Without realizing it, I absorbed so much information from Mom and her friends that they still, to this day, inspire how I cook for my family and friends. I remember having lemon sorbet for the first time and learning it was not, in fact, a dessert, but a palate cleanser between courses. That early taste memory was the inspiration for my Yuzu Citrus Sorbet (page 138; I definitely encourage you to have it for dessert!). I learned that in Japanese cooking, it's important to "eat with your eyes." In our culture, food presentation is just as important as preparation. I learned to make colorful dishes that are pleasing to look at as well as delicious. The Dames taught me that sometimes the finishing touch is a sprig of bamboo from the garden or a gardenia and some greenery on a dessert tray. When I looked at the food spread across the table, it made me feel special, like I was part of a secret club or eating at one of the best restaurants in town.

While working on my first cookbook, *Simply Ramen*, I started gathering ideas from a cookbook called *Les Dames* that The Dames wrote back in 1992. It is such a testament to their time (you'll find baby back ribs next to beef shabu-shabu) that it's now sold at the Japanese American National Museum in Los Angeles. The recipes in *Simply Ramen* are easy to follow with accessible ingredients and are a perfect amalgam of Japanese and American cultures. In that book, I explored traditional and nontraditional ways of making ramen. In this book I follow the same format, giving you the foundation to make traditional Japanese hot pots with a variety of basic broth recipes and also some international favorites. Some recipes use a classic Japanese broth that might be put to use in a modern way, such as my Slow-Cooked Beef Brisket in Tomato Broth — an ode to my Jewish mother-in-law.

What is hot pot cooking? It's about bringing people together. It's comfort food. It's healthy, affordable, quick and easy. It's a complete one-pot meal that can be customized for anyone. Hot pot cooking embodies Asian culture with its use of fresh, seasonal ingredients, delicate presentation, and the humble manner in which it is served. In Japan, hot pots are called *nabemono* (nah-beh-mo-no), or *nabe* for short. The stout, clay, lidded pots that nabe are cooked in are called *donabe* (doh-nah-beh; directly translated, *nabe* means "pot"). They have not changed for generations and continue to be a fixture in today's Japanese kitchen. A typical hot pot meal in Japan has a family gathered around the dining table with a donabe of bubbling dashi broth as the centerpiece. There are overflowing plates of thinly sliced beef, bite-size squares of creamy tofu, fresh chrysanthemum leaves and piles of Napa cabbage, tender shiitake mushrooms, colorful carrots and julienned scallion — all ready to take a short dip in the warm broth. A small bowl of zesty ponzu sauce is served on the side as a dip for the meat and vegetables. The meal ends with a *shime* (she-meh), or end-of-meal course, such as a pile of plump udon noodles, placed into the broth once the meat and vegetables have been eaten, and simmered until warm and brimming with the broth's delicate flavor. Conversation slows as everyone sits back, slurps their noodles and feels full and satisfied.

Although the majority of recipes in this book are Japanese-inspired, hot pots are found all over Asia — from Korea to Thailand. I've included a few of my favorites to show not only the versatility and universality of this type of cooking, but also because I'm a huge fan of the international broths filled with aromatics and herbs. You'll quickly find that once you master the Hot Pot Basics (see page 16), it is easy to experiment within these recipes and make them your own, whether it's using what's in your refrigerator, playing with protein choices, or amping up the spiciness of your broth to your liking. For each recipe, I've chosen a broth with proteins and vegetables that I think pair well, but you will soon realize these recipes are merely templates for your own explorations. You'll also find sauces to go alongside the hot pots, plus some traditional (and nontraditional) side dishes and desserts.

I cook with traditional Asian ingredients as much as possible, but out of necessity, I also use what is readily available where I currently live, in Boulder, Colorado. I want my cookbook to inspire people to learn more about Asian cooking and culture, and not be intimidated by ingredients they can't find, or techniques that seem unfamiliar or too challenging. Since my family and I moved from the Bay Area in Northern California, I have found the availability of Asian and Japanese ingredients to be a bit more limited. When I was developing recipes for this book, I really put thought into substitutes for ingredients that can be found in most grocery stores or online, so you can still make the recipe even if you can't find the ingredients in your area. If you are lucky enough to live near an Asian market or a Japantown, use it as a cultural adventure to seek out the best of what's in season or take your kids and educate them on the many different types of basic hot pot ingredients, such as mushrooms, tofu, greens and noodles.

For my family, hot pot nights are when we're excited to come to the table to share our day with each other and cook together, as everyone picks what they like and adds it to the pot. My hope is for you to do the same with your family and friends. Please join me on my continuing journey to preserve my family history through food, and thank you for letting me show you how to make Japanese- and Asian-inspired hot pots in your own home. Even though I may not know you personally, we are now connected through food. Enjoy!

—Amy Kimoto-Kahn

Mussels in Spicy Tomato Broth, page 108

Hot Pot Equipment

One of the benefits of hot pot cooking is that you probably have everything you need in your kitchen already. Asian-style hot pot cooking is not pretentious — it's casual and more about bringing people together. If you don't have a traditional clay pot, use what you have, be it an enameled cast-iron casserole or a deep skillet. If you find that you really enjoy hot pot cooking, treat yourself to a clay pot. These glazed pots come in different styles, so take your time looking for one you like. While hot pot cooking is not about having state-of-the-art equipment, there are a few utensils, pieces of equipment and cooking vessels I will describe — both traditional and nontraditional — that will help you achieve the best results.

THE DONABE CLAY POT

This is the traditional Japanese clay pot commonly used for hot pots or to steam vegetables or rice, or to roast meats. The special clay used to make a donabe conducts heat evenly throughout the surface of the pot and retains that heat even when the temperature is lowered, keeping food warm for a lengthy period.

All donabe come with a lid that has a hole to let steam escape, which also helps regulate the heat. The special clay of a donabe also helps the heat build slowly, which keeps food from burning. Hot pot cooking is all about slowly building flavor over time. A traditional Japanese donabe is best used over an open flame on a gas stovetop or a portable gas burner. The flames surround the bottom of the donabe and build heat evenly. (A donabe should not be used on an electric or portable electric stove, to avoid uneven distribution of heat.)

When looking for a donabe, a handcrafted one can last a lifetime. Look for one made with coarse clay that has been fired twice. Get one that suits your family's size or entertaining habits — I personally like the larger 4-quart (3.8 L) ones because they are big enough to feed my whole family and any extra guests. My favorite donabe is one I purchased at toirokitchen.com, a great online shop for donabe ware. It's the large Mushi Nabe and comes with a steamer attachment. I like its versatility — I can use it to cook rice and steam vegetables, as well as to prepare hot pots. Plus, it's big enough that I can easily cook hot pots for up to eight people.

To prolong your donabe's life, it needs to be cured. The naturally porous clay has small holes that must be sealed to prevent leakage and excessive cracking. This process, called *medome*, involves cooking rice in water until the starches fill the microscopic pores of the pot — this not only helps prevent breakage and heat damage, but also prevents smells and stains from food that might permeate into the pores of the pot when cooked. Unlike a wok or cast-iron skillet, you do not want the donabe to take on the flavors of the ingredients cooked in it. You'll find a simple method for curing your donabe overleaf.

CURING YOUR DONABE CLAY POT

1 Prepare a mixture of about 80 percent water to 20 percent short-grain Japanese rice. (The amounts will vary depending on the size of your donabe.) Add water to the donabe until it's about three-quarters full. Add rice to about a quarter of the water's height. Gently rub together the rice and water with your hands until the water looks milky. Do not drain the water.

2 Cover the donabe and place it over medium-high heat. Bring the water and rice to a slow boil. Remove the cover, reduce the heat to low and simmer for 1 hour to 1 hour 30 minutes, stirring occasionally, until most of the water has evaporated and the rice looks like a paste.

3 After this paste-like consistency is achieved, turn off the heat and let cool for about 1 hour 30 minutes. Discard the rice mixture. Rinse and dry the donabe. It's now ready to use.

ELECTRIC HOT POTS

An electric hot pot is a great alternative to a donabe for the modern family. It's best used when you are making hot pots at the table — where meat and vegetables are arranged on platters so everyone can cook their own food. Electric hot pots also have an adjustable temperature control so the heat can be easily regulated throughout the cooking process. I own the Zojirushi Gourmet 1350-Watt Electric Skillet, which is a nice large size, but also light enough to store and remove from the cupboard easily.

CAST IRON POTS

Cast-iron casseroles, skillets or enameled cast-iron braisers, such as the Le Creuset brand, are great for hot pot cooking, because they distribute heat efficiently like a clay donabe. The only downsides to keep in mind are that cast iron gets hot more quickly than a donabe and it doesn't retain heat for as long. A cast-iron hot pot also doesn't have a lid with a hole, but the same function can be achieved by placing the pot's lid a little askew for steam to escape. They are still a much better alternative to stainless steel, which does not conduct heat as evenly or protect your food as well from burning.

SPLIT HOT POTS

I've only been able to find aluminum split hot pots; I do not believe there is a clay donabe that has a split option. That said, these are great when you want to offer both a spicy and a nonspicy version of a base broth, like in my Mongolian Broth (page 33).

RICE COOKERS

If you own a rice cooker, you know how essential it is. It makes cooking rice easy and fail-safe, giving you light, fluffy rice every time. Most rice cookers also have a warming function, so you can make the rice before your company arrives, and it will be hot and ready to eat when you need it. In my opinion, Japanese models are superior because they have more settings to choose from specifically for Japanese rice, such as regular white short-grain rice, sushi rice, semi-brown rice, and porridge settings. I'm a big fan of the Zojirushi brand. We eat a lot of rice in our home, so we have the 5½-cup (1.3 L) capacity, but they are available in smaller and larger sizes.

Crab Legs and Tofu in
Pork Bone Broth, page 86

Mixed Vegetables in
Soy Milk Broth, page 98

PRESSURE COOKERS

If you plan to make your own bone broths — and I strongly encourage you to, as the quality is incomparable — you'll need a pressure cooker, which makes the process easier and faster. I've found that a 30-quart (29 L) pressure cooker yields about 3 quarts (2.9 L) of rich, unctuous bone broth. You can purchase a smaller model (that will take up less space), but this is a project that requires an afternoon, so you might as well make enough broth to freeze and last a while. The other option is to use an Instant Pot or other electric pressure cooker and make your bone broth in two or three batches, or make the broth in a large stockpot and cook it over low heat for 15 to 20 hours.

PORTABLE BURNERS

A clay donabe should not be used on an electric stovetop to avoid uneven distribution of heat and scorching your food. They are best used over an open gas flame, so the flame can surround the bottom of the donabe and build heat evenly. If you plan to cook your hot pot at the table and have everyone help themselves, a portable gas burner is very convenient. I like the Iwatani 35FW Portable Butane Stove because it's fairly compact and you can set it directly on a wood table without fear of it causing any damage. I recommend buying extra butane cartridges, but one cartridge will last through two to three hot pots.

SIEVES

A couple of fine-mesh sieves are must-haves for hot pot cooking so that it's easy to retrieve protein and veggies from the broth easily. Because a dipping sauce is often served with hot pots, you want the food to be free from liquid so it can soak up all the flavor of the dipping sauce without diluting it.

SERVING CHOPSTICKS

Long chopsticks allow people to sit around the table and add food to the hot pot themselves, even when not within easy reach of the broth. Longer chopsticks allow people to do this without standing up, and it makes it easier to put food into and take it out of the pot.

A SHARP CHEF'S KNIFE

If you cannot find frozen presliced shabu-shabu–style meat (very thinly sliced meat, about $\frac{1}{8}$ inch [3 mm] or thinner) at your Asian market or have your butcher slice it for you, a sharp chef's knife is essential for slicing the meat at home. The trick is to freeze the meat for up to 4 hours, until it is firm and easier to slice. If you are slicing fish, just refrigerate it overnight until firm. I prefer the forged steel blade of a Japanese knife because it retains its edge longer. Shun is a great brand, widely available in the United States.

PLATTERS

Use any large platter, be it round, oblong, or rectangular, for setting your table. A mixture of platters creates a beautiful presentation, so don't feel that they all need to match. I like to separate my meats and seafood from the vegetables to reduce the risk of salmonella. Try arranging everything with a variety of color and texture to make it pleasing to the eye.

Hot Pot Basics

What makes hot pots so simple and delicious is that they all have the same basic components: a base broth, proteins and vegetables, noodles and/or rice, garnishes and sauces. Here, I outline some of my favorites in each category, as well as a description of why each is used. Remember that any recipe can be made with substitutes if you can't find the specific ingredients in your local area (substitutions are in parentheses after the recommended ingredients). I have also included a glossary of Asian hot pot ingredients (page 20) for your reference.

The method for cooking, whether stovetop or at the table, depends on the cooking time for your ingredients. (The preferred cooking method is noted for each hot pot recipe in this book.) If you are using thinly sliced pieces of meat and vegetables that only need to simmer for 1 to 2 minutes in the base broth (like with my Rib Eye Shabu-Shabu, page 57), I recommend cooking at the table. If you are cooking larger pieces of chicken with thicker pieces of kabocha pumpkin and eggplant, for instance, I recommend cooking on the stovetop, like with my Thai Coconut Curry Chicken Hot Pot (page 110). Sukiyaki, a very traditional type of Japanese hot pot, can use either of these methods, but I prefer to cook it at the table, where small batches of meat can be poached quickly, like with my Pork Sukiyaki (page 70) and Wagyu Beef Sukiyaki (page 58).

As you learn more about hot pot assembly, you will be able to pick a favorite base broth and then choose a hot pot cooking method that best suits it. Regardless of the method you choose, what's most important is to enjoy the process and experiment — there is no right or wrong way, as long as you are taking pleasure in the company of family and friends.

THE BASE BROTH

Your base broth is the foundation for the flavor layering that will be fortified by the ingredients that are added. Traditional Japanese broth is made with dashi stock (a combination of water, kombu seaweed and bonito fish flakes), but more strongly flavored broths, such as soy milk and miso are also used, as well as more viscous broths, such as a chicken or pork-bone broth.

MAIN INGREDIENTS (PROTEINS)

Your protein choice can really change the flavor of your base broth. Chicken tends to give a lighter, more savory flavor; beef, pork, or duck are richer; and seafood imparts a salty brininess. I've been lucky enough to find all my proteins in thinly sliced form at Asian markets. My favorite is wagyu beef because of how tender it stays regardless of cooking time and how well it pairs with sauces.

GREENS

Greens add color, flavor and texture to the broth and they balance the mellowness of other vegetables. They are great for dipping into sauces. Shungiku chrysanthemum leaves and Napa cabbage are my favorite greens and are among the most popular hot pot ingredients.

MUSHROOMS

Mushrooms provide a meatier texture to the hot pot, round out the earthier flavors of the broth

with their umami goodness and add a visual balance. I'm a big fan of enoki mushrooms; they are light and delicate and cook up quickly. If you can find maitake mushrooms, they add a wonderful earthy flavor to any hot pot, and they have a beautiful, flowerlike appearance.

ONIONS

From sharp and acidic to sweet and mild, onions play an important role in hot pots, because their flavor and texture change with the length of time they are cooked, varying from crisp with more bite and flavor, or more mellow, blending with other ingredients. I prefer negi, or Japanese green onion, to any other onion because, when raw, it flavors the broth with a strong onion taste, but as it cooks it becomes milder and sweet, making it easy to eat in large amounts without being overpowering.

ROOTS AND TUBERS

When roots and tubers are cooked just right, they have a nice al dente feel to them. They pair well with proteins and make a hot pot heartier and more satisfying without making anything too heavy. I always take care not to cook them for too long because they can easily overcook and get mushy. I like kabocha Japanese pumpkin, because you can eat the peel and it tastes like both sweet potato and pumpkin.

VEGETABLES

Easy to add, veggies can really change the flavor of the broth, based on what you use. They balance the color and texture, and contribute the best of what's in season.

TOFU

Full of protein and nutrients, tofu is a star ingredient and great for soaking up the flavors of the broth. Different varieties are becoming more widely available in supermarkets, which makes it easy for you to incorporate tofu into your cooking. Most recipes in this book use firm tofu, but a firm silken tofu is my choice for hot pots, if you can get hold of it, because it has the creamy, melt-in-your-mouth texture of silken tofu but is firm enough to hold up when being handled with the rest of the hot pot ingredients.

RICE

Not just a filler side dish, steamed Japanese rice can make a hot pot go from good to great. The quality of rice can vary greatly, so look for a higher-end brand. Haiga rice, which is like a combination of white and brown rice, is one of my favorites for hot pot cooking be-

cause it has a delicious nutty flavor and really soaks up the broth when used for the shime (end-of-meal course, see page 8).

NOODLES

Noodles are a great addition to hot pots because Japanese varieties come in gluten-free and low-calorie versions. They are either added to the pot directly or can be eaten at the end of the meal. Udon noodles are very filling and soak up and get coated with the broth — these are my choice to mop up the last of the broth at the end of the meal.

GARNISHES

Garnishes should be chosen to match the main protein and vegetables being served. I always provide shichimi togarashi, a Japanese spice-blend condiment. Other condiments include sansho pepper powder for extra spice, thinly sliced scallion, grated daikon radish, minced chives, garlic chives or garlic flowers, toasted black and white sesame seeds and shredded nori seaweed.

SAUCES

The most traditional Japanese sauces are ponzu and sesame, but other international hot pots have a wide variety of sauces ranging from chili oil to peanut sauce.

EGGS

With Japanese hot pots, it is traditional to use a beaten egg as a dipping accompaniment to sukiyaki. Many restaurants cannot serve raw eggs, so it is not always provided. Raw whole eggs can be placed in hot pot broths to slowly cook until they are soft-boiled.

Serving Hot Pots at Home

The daily routine at my house is pretty casual, so we often eat hot pots, just as they do in Japan, where sharing a hot pot is a simple and humble dining experience to be enjoyed with your loved ones. The style of food offered for hot pots can range from relaxed and comforting to more elevated and refined, and the same goes for the tableware. If I am entertaining special guests or have relatives in town, I will pull out my favorite porcelain dishes for hot pot; however, you should never worry about having the most expensive china or the most ornate cooking pot. The simple, colorful display of vegetables and proteins on the table makes the presentation special and beautiful on its own.

Whether entertaining or enjoying a casual night at home with my family, there are a few basic rules that I always follow when setting my table for a hot pot meal. These rules aren't complicated or hard-and-fast, so feel free to adapt them to what suits you.

SETTING THE TABLE

I prefer eating hot pots at the table because I like watching my family select what they want to cook for themselves, and I'm tricked into feeling like I'm getting a little break from cooking. There are hands crossing, people dipping, conversation happening — it's almost chaotic, but in the best way.

If you are cooking your hot pot at the table, you should set the portable gas burner, electric hot pot, or hot plate for the hot pot in the center. You'll see everyone's eyes open wide and mouths start to water when they see the bounty of food laid out on platters in front of them! They'll want to dig in immediately, so it's good to turn the burner on low and preheat the broth so it's ready to turn up to a gentle boil right as everyone is sitting down. Each table setting should have the following:

- A shallow bowl or a small plate, depending on whether your hot pot has a broth you'd like to pour over the food when it is served.
- If serving rice, use small, individual bowls. Fill them with hot, fluffy rice right before everyone sits down. Place this at the top left of each setting.
- A napkin folded on the left side or tied in a neat knot and placed on each plate.
- Chopsticks in the center above the plate.

- A glass of cold ice water, especially if it's a spicy hot pot. Place it at the top right of the setting.
- Individual serving bowls for sauces. Place them on either side.

If serving hot pot at the table, arrange all the ingredients on platters. I like to pile each ingredient in a mound on the platter so you can see the contrasting colors. I also recommend separating raw meats from the vegetables, noodles and tofu, and placing them on different platters. Any food for the end-of-meal course, such as noodles or rice to be cooked in the leftover broth, can also be set out like this. Place these platters of ingredients on either side of the hot pot before cooking. Place any garnishes, such as fresh herbs or seasonings, within reach. Also, after years of wiping down a dirty table at the end of the night, I now like to place small plates on either side of the hot pot for setting long serving chopsticks, a sieve and a large spoon. (The serving chopsticks are helpful if you have a long table and someone at the end needs to reach the hot pot, and a sieve is a great way to get all the cooked meat and vegetables out of the broth.)

When I serve a hot pot that has been cooked on the stovetop, I bring the hot pot to the table to ladle the soup into everyone's bowls. Then I return the pot to the stovetop so it can simmer over very low heat and stay warm. If anyone is hungry for seconds, they can help themselves, keeping the meal relaxed and casual.

A Glossary of Asian Hot Pot Ingredients

Most of these ingredients can be found at Asian markets or online.

Aburaage deep-fried tofu is thinly sliced tofu that has been deep-fried until puffy and golden. It is perfect in hot pots because it stays moist and spongy in texture even when soaked in broth.

Adzuki beans: Sweet, small red beans used in many Japanese desserts and candies. Canned varieties are fine to use.

Bonito flakes: One of two ingredients used to make traditional Japanese-style dashi stock and an essential in any Japanese pantry. Although they are made from dried bonito fish, they are mild in flavor and can be used as a condiment.

Chinese broccoli: Also called gai lan, this vegetable has thick stems and dark green leaves, both of which are edible. Similar to Western broccoli in flavor, Chinese broccoli pairs well with fattier proteins as a nice contrast in texture. Use regular broccoli as a substitute.

Chrysanthemum leaves *see* Shungiku

Daikon radish: A large, long, white radish with a mellow flavor that is eaten raw, cooked, or pickled. It's normally quite large so you generally only need to use a portion of one daikon for hot pots. Grated daikon adds a slight spiciness to any dressing or sauce and can also be used alone as a condiment. Use Western radish as a substitute.

Daikon radish sprouts: Sprouts that grow from a daikon plant. They have a slightly peppery flavor and are often used in salads and soups and with sashimi. They can be eaten cooked or raw and can be added directly to a hot pot or used as a garnish.

Dashi stock: *Dashi* is the Japanese word for stock, and dashi stock is used as the base for many soups and dipping sauces. It is typically made with water, bonito flakes and kombu seaweed. It is a fundamental Japanese ingredient and can also be found in concentrated powders or tea bags (with no MSG) that you can easily mix with water.

Enoki mushrooms: Beautiful, stark-white mushrooms with long stems and tiny caps. They come in bunches attached at the bottom. They are mild in flavor and tender, yet hold up when cooked in broth. They go well with anything. If you can't find enoki mushrooms, use white button mushrooms as a substitute.

Furikake sprinkles: A Japanese seasoning, sold readymade, made up of seaweed, sesame seeds, sugar and salt. It's commonly sprinkled over rice.

Grilled tofu has been broiled for a few minutes until it develops a speckled brown appearance. You can make this on your own or purchase it already broiled. You may find it sold under its Japanese name, yakidofu.

Harusame noodles: Cellophane noodles made from potatoes and that look like translucent sticks. Most varieties need to be hydrated in lukewarm water for 10 minutes before being cooked briefly in the hot pot broth. If you can't find harusame noodles, you can use rice noodles as a substitute.

Kabocha pumpkin: Small and stout, with a dark green outside and bright orange-yellow flesh. Its taste is similar to a sweet potato. Kabocha peel tenderizes and is edible once cooked. Use sweet potato as a substitute.

Kamaboko fish cake: A processed fish product sold in a half-moon–shaped block and usually colored pink and white.

Katakuriko potato starch: A great gluten-free alternative to flour or cornstarch when baking or deep-frying. Use cornstarch as a substitute.

Kombu seaweed: A kind of kelp that is traditionally used in Japan in a thick, dried form to make dashi stock. Kombu should not be rinsed because the white powder on its surface is very flavorful.

Kurobuta pork: Pork from a Berkshire pig, kurobuta is highly marbled and tends to have darker, more flavorful meat. If you can't find kurobuta pork, use any other type of heritage-breed pork that is similarly juicy and tender.

Layu chili oil : A Japanese variety of a Chinese chili oil commonly used as a condiment to add spice to a dish. It is typically made from a sesame oil infused with chopped chili pepper and paprika, giving it a reddish tint.

Lotus root: Visually appealing, lotus root has tubular holes throughout, so when sliced, it is very attractive and decorative. Its taste and texture are similar to water chestnut and its crunch holds up well in hot pot broths.

Maitake mushrooms: Also known as hen-of-the-woods, maitake have ombré shades of brown and look like big, delicate flowers. They have a complex flavor that is fruity, earthy and spicy. A dried variety can also be used by rehydrating in warm water. Use oyster mushrooms as a substitute.

Matcha green tea powder: Rich in antioxidants, made from different Japanese shade-grown green tea leaves. Unlike traditional teas that need to brew in tea bags that are then removed, matcha tea is dissolved in hot water.

Mirin: Sweetened rice wine used only for cooking, in teriyaki sauce, marinades and dressings, or as an all-purpose replacement for sugar. Although mirin contains low amounts of alcohol, it is safe for use in children's dishes as there is normally a very small amount added.

Miso paste: Made with cooked soybeans that have been fermented with koji (the edible fungus used to make sake) and salt. In this book I two varieties,. **White miso**, milder and slightly sweet, is often used in dressings and sauces. **Red miso** is aged longer and is saltier. It is most commonly used in miso soup.

Mizuna leaves: With long stems and craggy leaves, mizuna is spicy but not overpowering and ideal in hot pots if you want an extra kick. It can be eaten raw or cooked. Use mustard greens or arugula as a substitute.

Mochi ovaletts and mochi rice cakes: These are made of rice flour and formed into patties. They can be eaten as a dessert or used in savory dishes and soups. Smaller mochi rice cakes are called mochi ovaletts. They tenderize when cooked and are used in hot pots to provide a texture variety and to soak up the broth.

Negi onions: Japanese green onions that are thicker, larger and more flavorful than Western scallions or green onions. They taste similar to a leek, but are sweeter when cooked.

Neri goma sesame paste: A Japanese puree of roasted sesame seeds that can be bought readymade. It is like tahini but has a stronger, richer sesame taste.

Nori seaweed: Dark greenish-purple paper-thin sheets of crispy seaweed that are sold in large squares. It can also be bought shredded.

Ponzu sauce: A citrus-based sauce, sold in bottles, commonly made with yuzu citrus and a soy-sauce base. It is typically used as a sauce for shabu-shabu hot pots but can also be used for marinating meat and as a dressing. You can also make your own ponzu; see recipe on page 36.

Ramen noodles: You can find fresh ramen noodles that cook up in about 2 minutes at your Asian market. You can also find fresh frozen ramen in various thicknesses. You may also be able to find fresh (unfrozen) ramen noodles in the refrigerator section. Some ramen restaurants may sell their fresh noodles to you if you ask.

Sake: You will find cooking sake at any Japanese market, but I recommend regular drinking sake for the recipes in this book. Choose any variety that you are happy to drink on its own!

Satsumaimo: A Japanese sweet potato with a dark purple skin and a creamy pale yellow interior from the Satsuma region of Japan. It is very sweet when baked, but, when used in hot pots and thinly sliced, it adds a nice balance to the savory cooking broths.

Shichimi togarashi: A Japanese spice-blend condiment containing various red peppers, black and white sesame seeds, poppy seeds, dried tangerine peel, nori seaweed or shiso leaf, and sansho pepper. It's a popular way to spice up hot pots.

Shiitake mushrooms: Rich, woody and intense in flavor, these umami-filled mushrooms are perfect for hot pots because they hold their own and impart flavor to any broth. The stems are very tough, so they are usually removed before use. Most recipes in this book call for fresh shiitake if you can get hold of them. If not, use rehydrated dried shiitake as a substitute, but as they're stronger in flavor and aroma, use fewer than called for.

Shimeji mushrooms: These petite mushrooms, also known as beech mushrooms, come in brown (buna) and white (ronfun) varieties. They grow in clumps that you can trim and pull apart. They are mild in flavor and have a tender texture. Use enoki mushrooms as a substitute.

Shio koji: An umami-rich condiment made from salt and rice that is fermented with koji (the fungus used to make miso and sake).

Shirataki noodles: Made from the konjac yam, shirataki noodles can be bought in black and white varieties, depending on the type of yam. They are sold dried or packaged in liquid, have relatively no flavor, are gluten-free and low in carbohydrates and calories. They are great for hot pots because they cook quickly and take on the flavor of any broth.

Shiso leaves: Also known as perilla. Part of the mint family, shiso has a frilly leaf that makes an attractive addition to any hot pot. It has a plum-like flavor and can be eaten raw or cooked, or used as a condiment.

Shungiku: Chrysanthemum leaves that taste a little sour and bitter. Their tough stems should be removed and they should only be lightly cooked to preserve their crispness. Use watercress as a substitute.

Shoyu koji: Also called soy sauce koji, this is a savory condiment made from soy sauce and rice that is fermented with koji (the edible fungus used to make miso and sake). You can find it at Asian markets and online

Soy sauce: Soy sauce is an essential ingredient in Japanese cooking. There are many varieties that can vary in flavor, aroma and quality, so seek out ones that are naturally brewed without any additives. I use Japanese soy sauce in all recipes in this book. It has a milder flavor than Chinese soy sauce.

Tofu (*see also* **Aburaage deep-fried tofu** *and* **grilled tofu**)**:** Made from pressed soybean curd and available in a variety of textures. **Firm tofu** has a firm texture and holds up well in hot pots, soups and stews.

Silken tofu is more delicate in texture, with a smoother mouthfeel. It cannot withstand much cooking, but is available in firmer varieties if you can find it.

Udon noodles: Made from wheat flour, udon are thick and white with a neutral flavor. They are available dry, but I prefer the fresh or precooked varieties. Udon are perfect for the end of a hot pot meal as they remain tender and their dense shape helps soak up any remaining broth.

Wagyu beef: Very high-end, tender, well-marbled beef. If you can't find it, use any other well-marbled, tender beef, such as Prime or Choice Angus beef.

Yuba: Made from the layers of skin forming on top of soy milk after it is simmered, yuba is available fresh or dried. If dried, soak it in water to rehydrate before use.

Yuzu citrus: Not like a lemon or a lime, the yuzu has its own distinct flavor and a very fragrant peel. It's zesty but not overpowering and is the main ingredient in ponzu sauce.

Broths, Bases, Sauces and More

Basic Dashi Stock

In the simplest terms, dashi is the Japanese word for stock. Dashi stock is the basis for a lot of Japanese cooking and is used in simmered dishes like stews and soups, in dressings and even in sauces. If you don't have time to make dashi from scratch, there are instant dashi products that can be decent substitutes. Kombu seaweed, sold in large dried pieces, is the main ingredient in dashi. It should be soaked in room-temperature water and boiled briefly. If boiled for too long, the kombu produces a slimy film you do not want in your dashi.

SKILL LEVEL: Easy
PREP TIME: 10 minutes, plus 3 hours soaking time
COOK TIME: 30 minutes
YIELD: Makes 2 quarts (1.9 L)

INGREDIENTS

2 pieces dried kombu, each 4 inches (10 cm)
10 cups (2.4 L) room-temperature water
6 cups loosely packed bonito flakes, about 2 ounces (55 g)

1 Using a damp cloth, wipe the kombu seaweed lightly to remove any dirt, but do not remove the white powdery coating, because this is what gives the dashi flavor.
2 Fill a large saucepan with the water and add the kombu. Let soak for 3 hours. Remove and discard the kombu.
3 Bring the water to a boil over medium-high heat, then reduce the heat to a low simmer. Add the bonito flakes. Simmer for 10 minutes.
4 Strain the stock through a fine-mesh sieve set over a large bowl, pressing on the solids to extract as much liquid as possible. Discard the bonito flakes.
5 Dashi can be refrigerated for up to 1 week or frozen for up to 1 month.

Chicken Stock

This chicken stock recipe uses wings and thighs because these dark meat cuts have more fat on them and impart better flavor to a stock. Rather than discarding the wings and thighs, I like to fry them up in a little bit of oil after making the broth and toss them in some teriyaki sauce.

SKILL LEVEL: Easy
PREP TIME: 10 minutes
COOK TIME: 3 to 4 hours
YIELD: Makes 10 cups (2.4 L)

INGREDIENTS

3 quarts (2.9 L) water
1 pound (450 g) chicken wings
1 pound (450 g) bone-in, skin-on chicken thighs
2 large scallions, white and light green parts, halved crosswise
1 tablespoon kosher salt

1 Fill a large stockpot with the water and bring to a boil.
2 Add the chicken wings and thighs, scallions and salt. Return the water to a boil, reduce the heat to low and simmer the broth, uncovered, until reduced slightly and flavorful, 3 to 4 hours. Skim off any scum that floats to the surface.
4 Remove the chicken and strain the liquid.
5 This stock can be made ahead and refrigerated for up to 1 week and frozen for up to 2 months.

Vegetable Stock

This all-purpose recipe is from my colleague Julia Heffelfinger, a pro recipe developer and editor. The addition of an apple is a trick of her mom, who adds a tart Honeycrisp apple (but any non-mealy apple will work) for a touch of sweetness to round out the earthy vegetables. Also, this stock is a great way to use up vegetable scraps. She keeps a large resealable plastic bag in her freezer. If she has carrot peel, parsley stems, mushroom stems, apple cores, or onion roots and peel, she sticks them in the bag. When it's full, she dumps it into a pot, covers everything with water and lets it simmer away.

SKILL LEVEL: Easy
PREP TIME: 30 minutes
COOK TIME: 3 to 4 hours
YIELD: Makes 10 cups (2.4 L)

INGREDIENTS

10 cups (2.4 L) water
4 celery ribs, coarsely chopped
2 large carrots, scrubbed and
   coarsely chopped
1 large yellow onion, unpeeled,
   halved
1 package cremini mushrooms, about
   8 ounces, or 220 g) cleaned
1 Honeycrisp apple, halved
1 head garlic, halved crosswise
1 small bunch fresh parsley
4 sprigs thyme
2 bay leaves

1 In a large stockpot, combine all the ingredients. Cover and bring to a boil.
2 Reduce the heat to low and simmer, partially covered, until very flavorful, 3 to 4 hours.
3 Strain the stock into a clean pot. Discard the vegetables and aromatics.
4 This stock can be made ahead and refrigerated for up to 1 week and frozen for up to 2 months.

Chicken Bone Broth

Homemade bone broth has a silky mouthfeel and gives your hot pot a rich chicken flavor, so if you have the time to make this, your hot pot will be better for it. The key here is using a pressure cooker (or an Instant Pot or other electric pressure cooker if you have one) because the steam inside the pot draws out the bone marrow, giving it an unctuous, slightly thick consistency and a creamy, opaque color.

SKILL LEVEL: Advanced
PREP TIME: 15 minutes
COOK TIME: 2 hours 30 minutes
YIELD: Makes 3 quarts (2.9 L)

EQUIPMENT

30-quart (29 L) pressure cooker (follow the manufacturer's instructions; if you do not have a pressure cooker this size, prepare this recipe in 2 or 3 batches in a smaller slow cooker or electric pressure cooker, such as an Instant Pot, or make it in a large stockpot and cook over low heat for 15 to 20 hours until the broth is a creamy white color and all the meat has fallen off the bones)

INGREDIENTS

1½ pounds (680 g) chicken wings and drumettes
6 pounds (2.7 kg) , skin-on, bone-in chicken thighs
2½ pounds (1.1 kg) chicken drumsticks
1 pound (450 g) potatoes, unpeeled, cut into large chunks
5 quarts (4.8 L) water

1 In a 30 quart (29 L) pressure cooker, combine the chicken wings and drumettes, thighs, drumsticks and potatoes. Cover with the water, making sure the total volume of water and ingredients does not exceed half the height of the pot.
2 Place the cover on the pressure cooker, leaving the pressure regulator weight off the vent pipe. Turn the heat to high until steam flows from the vent pipe (this may take up to 20 minutes) and continue to let vent for 10 minutes more while the steam displaces the air in the cooker. Place the regulator weight on the vent pipe and maintain a high heat setting. Start timing your cooking when the regulator weight begins to jiggle or rock. It may appear as if it is leaking, but this is normal. Regulate the heat so it maintains a temperature between 240°F and 250°F (115°C and 120°C). Start the timer and cook for 1 hour.
3 Turn off the heat and allow the pressure gauge to return to 0 (zero) before gently removing the cover. Push the chicken bones down to press out the fat, which will make the soup thicker and creamier.
4 Return the pressure cooker to medium-low heat. Cook for 1 hour more, uncovered, stirring occasionally, until the broth is creamy white and all the meat has fallen off the bones.
5 Turn off the heat. Remove all the larger bones. Using a large fine-mesh sieve set over a large stockpot, strain the remaining solids and discard them.
6 This broth can be made ahead and refrigerated for up to 3 days or frozen for up to 1 month.

Pork Bone Broth

This unctuous, creamy, fat-laden broth is one of my favorite hot pot broths — it's brimming with depth and layered flavor. This recipe does require a pressure cooker and some patience to break down the collagen in the pork bones, but the preparation is minimal and well worth the effort. Make this broth without the chili oil if you prefer a milder flavor or add more if you like some spiciness.

My sensei at ramen school taught me to pound the pork bones with a mallet to loosen the marrow so it melts right into the broth when you cook it — so don't skip this important step! Pressure cooking the pork pieces compresses the fat and bone marrow, making this broth incredibly silky and creamy in just 2 hours — versus 20 hours on the stovetop!

SKILL LEVEL: Advanced
PREP TIME: 25 minutes
COOK TIME: 3 hours
YIELD: Makes 3 quarts (2.9 L)

EQUIPMENT
30-quart (29 L) pressure cooker (read and follow the manufacturer's instructions; if you do not have a pressure cooker this size, prepare a half batch in an Instant Pot, but I do not recommend using a regular stockpot for this.)

INGREDIENTS
10 pounds (4.5 kg) pork knuckles or trotters, pounded with a mallet to release the marrow
¼ cup (60 ml) soy sauce
¼ cup (60 ml) mirin
1 teaspoon kosher salt
1 piece fresh ginger, about 1½ inches (3.5 cm), peeled and finely grated
½ teaspoon roasted chili oil, plus more as needed, optional

1 In a large stockpot over high heat, combine the pork bones with enough water to cover (roughly 5 quarts, or 4.8 L) and bring to a boil. Cook for 15 minutes, uncovered; drain well. Rinse the pork bones thoroughly to remove any scum.
2 Add the cleaned bones to a 30-quart (29 L) pressure cooker. Cover the bones with water (about 4 quarts, or 3.8 L), making sure the total volume of water and pork bones does not exceed half the height of the pot
3 Place the cover on the pressure cooker, leaving your pressure regulator weight off the vent pipe. Turn the heat to high until steam flows from the vent pipe (this may take up to 20 minutes) and continue to let it vent for 10 minutes more while the steam displaces the air in the cooker. Maintain a high heat and start timing your cooking when the regulator weight begins to jiggle or rock. It may seem to be leaking, but this is normal. Regulate the heat so the weight only jiggles 1 to 4 times per minute. Start the timer and cook for 1 hour.
4 Turn off the heat and allow the pressure gauge to return to 0 (zero) before gently removing the cover. Press down on the pork bones to get all the bone marrow out. Return the pressure cooker to medium-low heat and cook the broth for about 1 hour more, uncovered, stirring occasionally, until it is creamy and milky white.
5 Using a fine-mesh sieve set over a 4-quart (3.8 L) hot pot or large saucepan, strain the broth, pressing on the solids to extract as much liquid as possible. Discard the pork bones.
6 Whisk in the soy sauce, mirin, salt, ginger and chili oil (if using).
7 Use this broth immediately or let cool and refrigerate for up to 3 days or freeze for up to 1 month.

Basic Shabu-Shabu Broth

I love shabu-shabu–style hot pots because they can only be enjoyed communally and they please everyone — from my five-year-old to my husband. Shabu-shabu is an onomatopoeia for the sound the food makes when you swish it back and forth in the boiling broth. I giggle every time my kids say "shabu-shabu" while they swish their meat and vegetables around. Traditionally, this gentle wafting of meat is done in water only, and it's the ingredients you swish around in the water that add flavor. My version starts with chicken stock (or vegetable stock) and kombu seaweed because I think you end up with a more complex broth. The shime, or finish, of this meal is the best part for me simmering hot steamed rice or udon noodles in the delicious leftover broth after all the meat and vegetables are consumed. My favorite recipes that use this shabu-shabu broth are the Rib Eye Shabu-Shabu (page 57) and Seafood Medley Shabu-Shabu (page 89).

SKILL LEVEL: Easy
PREP TIME: 30 minutes
COOK TIME: 20 minutes
YIELD: Makes 2 quarts (1.9 L)

TO MAKE IN ADVANCE
Chicken Stock (page 26) or Vegetable Stock (page 27)

INGREDIENTS
2 quarts (1.9 L) Chicken Stock or Vegetable Stock, or store-bought low-sodium chicken or vegetable broth
2 pieces dried kombu, each 4 inches (10 cm)

1 In a 4-quart (3.8 L) hot pot or large saucepan, combine the chicken stock and kombu. Let the kombu soak in the stock for 30 minutes without heating.
2 Bring the chicken stock to a boil over medium-high heat. As soon as it reaches a boil, remove and discard the kombu. (Leaving the kombu in boiling water produces a slimy residue that will make the broth bitter.)
3 Use the broth at once or let cool and refrigerate until ready to use.
4 This broth can be made ahead and refrigerated for up to 1 week or frozen for up to 2 months.

Soy Milk Broth

This simple broth is heartwarming and creamy, but miraculously dairy-free because it contains soy milk. It pairs well with both proteins and vegetables and is a good match for almost any dipping sauce. I've made the spicy chili oil and the red pepper flakes optional, but they add a nice kick that complements the silky soy-milk base. Try this broth in my Chicken Hot Pot with Soy Milk (page 48) for something more similar to a stew, or my Mixed Vegetables in Soy Milk Broth (page 98) for a shabu-shabu–style hot pot brimming with veggies.

SKILL LEVEL: Easy
PREP TIME: 10 minutes
COOK TIME: 30 minutes
YIELD: Makes 2 quarts (1.9 L)

TO MAKE IN ADVANCE
Basic Dashi Stock (page 26)
Chicken Stock (page 26)

INGREDIENTS
3 cups (720 ml) unsweetened soy milk
2 cups (480 ml) Basic Dashi Stock, or dashi made with an instant mix
2 cups (480 ml) Chicken Stock, or store-bought low-sodium chicken broth
½ cup (130 g) white miso paste
½ cup (120 ml) sake
¼ cup (60 ml) soy sauce
½ teaspoon chili oil, optional
1 tablespoon red pepper flakes, optional

1 Heat a 4-quart (3.8 L) hot pot or large saucepan over medium-high heat (about 425°F, or 220°C, in an electric hot pot).
2 Add the soy milk, dashi, chicken stock, miso, sake and soy sauce. Bring to a boil, whisking occasionally, until everything is incorporated. If you like it spicy, add chili oil and red pepper flakes.
3 Cover, reduce the heat to low and simmer for 20 minutes to let the flavors develop.
4 This broth can be made ahead and refrigerated for up to 3 days or frozen for up to 1 month.

Creamy Corn Broth

This broth gets its silky texture and subtle sweetness from fresh corn, and its creaminess from the whole milk and heavy cream. It is best made when corn is at its peak, but you can make it year-round with frozen corn. I also like this hot pot because it's not too heavy. The chicken stock thins it out a bit and gives it the perfect consistency for hot pot cooking. This broth is not ideal for making ahead and freezing because of the dairy, but it cooks in about 30 minutes and is still easy to pull together on a weeknight.

SKILL LEVEL: Moderate
PREP TIME: 20 minutes
COOK TIME: 35 minutes
YIELD: Makes 2 quarts (1.9 L)

TO MAKE IN ADVANCE
Chicken Stock (page 26)

INGREDIENTS
2 tablespoons unsalted butter
1 medium Vidalia onion, chopped
3 cups (480 g) raw corn kernels
   (from about 4 cobs; or frozen
   corn kernels, thawed)
1 teaspoon freshly grated nutmeg
3 cups (720 ml) Chicken Stock,
   or store-bought low-sodium
   chicken broth
2 cups (480 ml) whole milk
1 cup (240 ml) heavy cream
¼ cup (70 g) white miso paste
1 teaspoon kosher salt
¼ teaspoon freshly ground black
   pepper

1 In a 4-quart (3.8 L) hot pot or large saucepan over medium-high heat (about 425°F, or 220°C, in an electric hot pot), melt the butter. Add the onion. Cook for about 10 minutes, stirring occasionally, until translucent.
2 Add the corn and nutmeg. Cook for about 10 minutes, until the corn is just tender.
3 Stir in the remaining ingredients and bring to a boil. Cover the pot, reduce the heat to low and simmer until the broth is very flavorful, about 10 minutes.
4 Scrape the broth into a blender and puree until smooth or use an immersion blender right in the pot.
5 Use this broth for a hot pot or enjoy on its own.

Japanese Curry Broth

Like most Japanese, I grew up eating Japanese curry out of a box with roux cubes you added to hot water. Although I have fond memories of those curried stews, I wanted to try a Japanese-style curry from scratch with freshly toasted spices and aromatics, such as garlic and ginger. Japanese curries are different from other curries because they are less spicy and have a subtle sweetness that kids tend to like (my kid-friendly Beef Curry Hot Pot on page 64 will please even the pickiest kids).

This broth gets its rich color and depth from caramelized onion and a toasty roux that has a touch of bitter espresso powder mixed in. A roux is a combination of fat and flour (in this case, we use butter) used to thicken broth. The coffee flavor is very subtle, but it goes well with fattier cuts of meat such as beef. I use dark brown sugar as it gives a darker color and richer flavor to the broth than regular brown sugar. Traditional Japanese curry is thicker than this broth, but I've made it intentionally thinner so you can use it as a hot pot base.

SKILL LEVEL: Moderate
PREP TIME: 20 minutes
COOK TIME: 1 hour
YIELD: Makes 2 quarts (1.9 L)

TO MAKE IN ADVANCE
Chicken Stock (page 26)

INGREDIENTS
1 tablespoon olive oil
2 large garlic cloves, minced
1 piece fresh ginger, about 1 inch (2.5 cm),
   peeled and finely grated
1 medium sweet onion, thinly sliced
¼ cup (½ stick, or 50 g) unsalted butter
¼ cup (30 g) all-purpose flour
2 tablespoons curry powder
1 tablespoon garam masala
¼ teaspoon instant espresso powder (not
   ground; needs to be powder)

¼ teaspoon ground white pepper
¼ cup (60 ml) soy sauce
¼ cup (60 g) packed dark brown sugar
2 tablespoons tomato paste
5 cups (1.2 L) Chicken Stock, or store-bought low-sodium chicken broth

1 In a 4-quart (3.8 L) hot pot or large saucepan over medium-high heat (about 425°F, or 220°C, in an electric hot pot), heat the olive oil. Add the garlic and ginger. Cook for about 2 minutes, stirring occasionally, until fragrant.
2 Add the onion. Reduce the heat to medium. Cook for about 20 minutes, stirring and scraping up any brown bits from the bottom of the pot, until the onion starts to caramelize. Using a slotted spoon, transfer the onion and aromatics to a small bowl. Set aside.
3 In the same pot over medium heat, melt the butter. Add the flour. Cook for about 5 minutes, stirring constantly with a wooden spoon until you have a roux that is pale brown in color and smells nutty.
4 Stir in the curry powder, garam masala, espresso powder and white pepper. Continue to cook until fragrant and a deep brown, about 2 minutes.
5 Return the onion and aromatics to the pot. Stir in the soy sauce, brown sugar, tomato paste and chicken stock. Bring the broth to a boil.
6 Cover the pot, reduce the heat to low and simmer for about 20 minutes, until the broth is thickened slightly and is very flavorful.
7 This broth can be made ahead and refrigerated for up to 1 week or frozen for up to 2 months.

Thai Coconut Curry Broth

This soup has many layers: the creamy coconut milk soothes the complex curry paste, the brininess from the fish sauce gives it all the salt you need, and the pineapple and lychee make it slightly sweet and sour. This soup base is very versatile, plus it is gluten-free, low-carb and paleo. With the option to make it vegetarian by swapping out vegetable stock for the chicken, it can please anyone. For this reason, I like to make it ahead and keep it refrigerated for quick, flavorful meals. On a busy weeknight, I serve it poured over a hot bowl of steamed rice, garnished with a mess of fresh herbs. If you're looking for something heartier, try the Thai Coconut Curry Chicken Hot Pot (page 110) or get your mushroom fill with my Mixed Mushroom and Vegetable Hot Pot (page 101).

SKILL LEVEL: Moderate
PREP TIME: 20 minutes
COOK TIME: 30 minutes
YIELD: Makes 2 quarts (1.9 L)

TO MAKE IN ADVANCE
Chicken Stock (page 26)
Vegetable Stock (page 27)

INGREDIENTS
1 tablespoon vegetable oil
2 tablespoons red curry paste
3¼ cups (800 ml) full-fat coconut milk
1 quart (960 ml) Chicken Stock or Vegetable Stock, or store-bought low-sodium chicken broth or vegetable broth
6 small canned lychees, finely chopped
¼ cup (40 g) finely chopped pineapple

1½ tablespoons fish sauce
1 tablespoon grated palm sugar, or light brown sugar
4 kaffir lime leaves
1 teaspoon kosher salt

1 In a 4-quart (3.8 L) hot pot or large saucepan over medium-high heat (about 425°F, or 220°C, in an electric hot pot), heat the vegetable oil. Add the curry paste. Cook for about 2 minutes, stirring, until fragrant.
2 Stir in the coconut milk, chicken stock, lychees, pineapple, fish sauce, sugar, lime leaves and salt. Bring to a boil.
3 Cover the pot, reduce the heat to low and simmer for about 20 minutes, until very flavorful.
4 This broth can be made ahead and refrigerated for up to 3 days or frozen for up to 1 month.

Sesame Miso Broth

If you are in a rush, this recipe can be made with dashi from a powder or liquid concentrate and with ready- ground and toasted sesame seeds. I use both white and red miso here because white miso has a sweeter taste and red miso is stronger, which balances the broth. If you like a spicy broth, I suggest starting with a very small amount of chili oil and adding more according to your taste preference.

SKILL LEVEL: Moderate
PREP TIME: 10 minutes
COOK TIME: 30 minutes
YIELD: Makes 2 quarts (1.9 L)

TO MAKE IN ADVANCE
Basic Dashi Stock (page 26)

INGREDIENTS
1 cup (140 g) white sesame seeds
2 tablespoons sesame oil
2 large garlic cloves, minced
1 piece fresh ginger, about 1½ inches (3.5 cm), peeled and finely grated
2 quarts (1.9 L) Basic Dashi Stock, or dashi made with an instant mix
½ cup (120 ml) sake
½ cup (130 g) white miso paste
½ cup (130 g) red miso paste
Roasted chili oil, to taste, optional

1 In a small dry skillet over low heat, toast the sesame seeds for about 10 minutes, until fragrant and golden brown, constantly stirring or swirling the seeds in the pan as they cook. Let cool, then transfer to a mortar with a pestle or clean coffee grinder. Crush the toasted sesame seeds into a fine powder (see Tip, below).
2 In a 4-quart (3.8 L) hot pot or large saucepan over medium-high heat (about 425°F, or 220°C, in an electric hot pot), heat the sesame oil until shimmering.
3 Add the garlic and ginger. Cook for 1 minute until fragrant.
4 Stir in the dashi, sake, white and red miso pastes and ground sesame seeds. Add the chili oil if you like it spicy. Bring the mixture to a boil, reduce the heat to low and simmer for 10 minutes. If the broth evaporates too much while cooking and becomes thick, add more dashi — if you do not have any dashi on hand, water is also fine.
5 This broth can be made ahead and refrigerated for up to 3 days or frozen for up to 1 month.

TIP If you use a coffee grinder, be careful not to overprocess the seeds or you'll end up with sesame paste. Stop grinding before the seeds start to release oil or the powder will clump.

Tomato Broth

I like this broth because it holds its own even without being incorporated into a hot pot — the aromatics of the fennel, cinnamon and cumin really deepen the flavor of the tomato and make this a comforting dish on a cold winter's day. Finely chopping all the vegetables will fill every spoonful with added texture and flavor. If you have a food processor, make your life easier and just throw everything in there in big chunks and pulse away.

SKILL LEVEL: Moderate
PREP TIME: 20 minutes
COOK TIME: 30 minutes
YIELD: Makes 2 quarts (1.9 L)

TO MAKE IN ADVANCE
Vegetable Stock (page 27)

INGREDIENTS
1 tablespoon vegetable oil
1 medium red bell pepper, finely chopped
½ medium sweet onion, finely chopped
2 celery ribs, finely chopped
1 medium carrot, finely grated
2 large garlic cloves, finely grated
½ teaspoon ground fennel seeds
½ teaspoon ground cinnamon
½ teaspoon ground cumin
1 teaspoon kosher salt
½ teaspoon freshly ground black pepper
1 teaspoon fresh lemon thyme, or fresh regular thyme
2 bay leaves
2 cans tomato sauce, 8 ounces (220 g) each
6 cups (1.4 L) Vegetable Stock, or store-bought low-sodium vegetable broth
½ teaspoon roasted chili oil and ½ teaspoon red pepper flakes, plus more as needed, optional

1 In a 4-quart (3.8 L) hot pot or large saucepan over medium-high heat (about 425°F, or 220°C, in an electric hot pot), heat the vegetable oil. Add the red bell pepper, onion, celery, carrot and garlic. Cook for 10 minutes, stirring, until softened and the onion is translucent.
2 Stir in the fennel seeds, cinnamon, cumin, salt and pepper. Cook for 2 minutes.
3 Add the thyme, bay leaves, tomato sauce and vegetable stock. Bring the mixture to a boil. If you like it spicy, stir in the chili oil and red pepper flakes.
4 Cover the pot, reduce the heat to low and simmer for about 10 minutes, until very flavorful. Remove and discard the bay leaves before using as your hot pot base.
5 This broth can be made ahead and refrigerated for up to 3 days or frozen for up to 1 month.

Mongolian Broth

This deeply aromatic, luxurious broth was inspired by the well-known Mongolian hot pot chain, Little Sheep Hot Pot. Try my Mongolian Lamb Hot Pot (page 106), which incorporates both the original and the spicy versions of this broth. Unlike Japanese hot pots, Mongolian broth is laden with different aromatics and spices, such as black cardamom pods and dried goji berries, that make it so rich and savory, you'll want to save it for a cold day and sip it down all on its own. The skill level on this recipe is advanced because, although the techniques are fairly simple, many of the ingredients can be difficult to find. While most can be purchased at Asian specialty food markets or online, it does require extra time for sourcing (however, it's worth the effort!). The bone broth is what gives it an unctuous texture, so it's best not to substitute regular broth.

SKILL LEVEL: Advanced
PREP TIME: 20 minutes
COOK TIME: 20 minutes
YIELD: Makes 2 quarts (1.9 L)

TO MAKE IN ADVANCE
Chicken Bone Broth (page 27)

INGREDIENTS
ORIGINAL VERSION
9 cups (2.1 L) Chicken Bone Broth, or store-bought chicken bone broth
20 garlic cloves, peeled and crushed
2 negi Japanese green onions, or 4 large scallions, coarsely chopped
1 piece fresh ginger, about 5 inches (13 cm) peeled and thinly sliced
10 whole cloves
6 dried jujubes (red dates)
6 star anise
4 black cardamom pods
4 dried bay leaves
4 dried astragalus root slices
¼ cup (8 g) dried lotus seeds
2 tablespoons dried goji berries
1½ teaspoons kosher salt
1 teaspoon cumin seeds
¼ teaspoon ground white pepper

SPICY VERSION (SEE TIP, BELOW)
12 Chinese dried red chili peppers, halved
1 teaspoon Chinese chili powder, or red pepper flakes
Chili oil, to taste

TIP The ingredient amounts for the Spicy Version are for half a batch as you will be splitting the Original Version between two pots. If you want to make a full batch of spicy broth, double the Spicy Version ingredients.

1 Heat a hot pot or large saucepan over medium-high heat (about 425°F, or 220°C, in an electric pot). If making both broths, heat a split hot pot or 2 medium saucepans over medium-high heat.
2 To make the Original Version: Put all the ingredients in the pot. If making both broths, divide the ingredients equally between the two pots.
3 To make the Spicy Version: Add the chilis, chili powder and chili oil to the pot.
4 Increase the heat to high and bring the broth(s) to a boil.
5 Cover the pot(s), reduce the heat to low and simmer for about 10 minutes, until fragrant and very flavorful. Do not strain the aromatics from the broth.
6 This broth can be made ahead and refrigerated for up to 3 days or frozen for up to 1 month.

Vietnamese Broth

Every two weeks I go to this amazing Vietnamese eyelash technician, named Alice, who works out of her house. When I walk in the door I always find myself drifting toward the mouthwatering smells wafting from her kitchen. The air is filled with scents of star anise, fish sauce, fresh basil and lemongrass — it's her adorable mother who's always cooking away in the kitchen. I asked her how she makes her Vietnamese hot pot broth, and she told me it's very simple: chicken stock, tomatoes, lemongrass and fish sauce. She inspired me to make this hot and sour broth with spicy tom yum paste and flecks of sweet pineapple (another tip I learned from her). Try it as the base for my Vietnamese Oxtail Hot Pot (page 112). The tempting aroma is sure to draw curious guests to your kitchen too.

SKILL LEVEL: Moderate
PREP TIME: 20 minutes
COOK TIME: 30 minutes
YIELD: Makes 2 quarts (1.9 L)

TO MAKE IN ADVANCE
Chicken Stock (page 26)

INGREDIENTS
1 tablespoon vegetable oil
1 small Vidalia onion, thinly sliced
1 large tomato, cut into ½-inch-thick
 (1 cm) wedges
3 quarts (2.9 L) Chicken Stock, or
 store-bought low-sodium chicken
 broth
5 kaffir lime leaves
3 lemongrass stalks, tough outer
 layers removed, cut into 4-inch (10
 cm) pieces and crushed
½ cup (80 g) finely chopped
 pineapple
¼ cup (70 g) tom yum paste (see
 Tip, below)
1 tablespoon grated palm sugar, or
 light brown sugar
1 teaspoon fish sauce

TIP Tom yum paste is typically made from lemongrass, shallots, garlic, kaffir lime leaves, galangal, lime juice, fish sauce, red pepper flakes and soybean oil. There are multiple varieties, so look for one rich in color and made in Thailand. You can find it at Asian markets and online.

1 In a 4-quart (3.8 L) hot pot or large saucepan over medium-high heat (about 425°F, or 220°C, in an electric pot), heat the vegetable oil. Add the onion and tomato. Cook for about 5 minutes, stirring, until the onion is translucent and the tomato is softened.

2 Add the chicken stock, lime leaves, lemongrass, pineapple, tom yum paste, sugar and fish sauce. Increase the heat to high and bring to a boil.

3 Cover the pot, reduce the heat to low and simmer for about 20 minutes, until aromatic and very flavorful. Do not strain the aromatics from the broth.

4 This broth can be made ahead and refrigerated for up to 3 days. Gently reheat on the stovetop.

Kimchi Broth

Traditional Korean kimchi is a condiment made from vegetables — typically cabbage — fermented with ingredients such as fish sauce, garlic, chili pepper, ginger and salt. It has a layered, spicy kick that gives this broth its complexity. Also, the great part about kimchi is you can often find really good premade, organic (and local!) brands at your grocery store. When choosing, look for vibrant color, freshness of vegetables, and no additives like MSG. Kimchi tends to have a lot of zest, so I've added mirin and miso as my Japanese twist to give it some sweet and savory flavors. This broth is vegetarian, so you can use it as a base for any vegetarian hot pot. Or, if you enjoy meat, try my delicious Korean Short Ribs in Kimchi Broth (page 115) using this broth.

SKILL LEVEL: Easy
PREP TIME: 20 minutes
COOK TIME: 40 minutes
YIELD: Makes 2 quarts (1.9 L)

TO MAKE IN ADVANCE
Chicken Bone Broth (page 27)

INGREDIENTS
1 tablespoon vegetable oil
3 to 5 dried chili peppers of your choice, halved with seeds (depending on your heat preference)
½ medium sweet onion, thinly sliced
10 cups (2.4 L) Vegetable Stock, or store-bought low-sodium vegetable broth; substitute anchovy stock if available and you're not concerned with having a vegetarian broth
1 pound (450 g) kimchi with juices
6 tablespoons distilled white vinegar
3 tablespoons sugar
2 tablespoons gochujang (Korean red chili paste)
2 tablespoons red miso paste
2 tablespoons mirin
1 tablespoon sesame oil
1 tablespoon soy sauce

1 In a 4-quart (3.8 L) hot pot or large saucepan over medium-high heat (about 425°F, or 220°C, in an electric hot pot), heat the vegetable oil. Add the dried chilis. Cook for about 1 minute, stirring, until fragrant. Add the onion. Cook for about 5 minutes, stirring, until translucent.
2 Stir in the vegetable stock, kimchi and its juices, vinegar, sugar, gochujang, miso, mirin, sesame oil and soy sauce. Increase the heat to high and bring the broth to a boil.
3 Cover the pot, reduce the heat to low and simmer for about 30 minutes, until fragrant and very flavorful.
4 This broth can be made ahead and refrigerated for up to 3 days or frozen for up to 1 month.

Macanese Broth

This broth was created by my friend and chef Emily Lai. Macanese cuisine is from Macau, with its Portuguese and Chinese influences; its characteristic dishes are rich and multilayered with spices and aromatics — and this broth is no exception. The jujubes and goji berries provide a subtle sweetness and lend a fresh, floral note. (Bonus: now that you have these ingredients on hand, you can use them in my Mongolian Lamb Hot Pot (page 106) as well!) This hot pot base works well with shabu-shabu–style sliced meat and ingredients like mung bean noodles and yuba (tofu skin) — see Emily's Meat Lover's Macanese Hot Pot (page 62).

SKILL LEVEL: Moderate
PREP TIME: 10 minutes
COOK TIME: 3 hours 30 minutes
YIELD: Makes 2 quarts (1.9 L)

INGREDIENTS
5 pounds (2.3 kg) pork bones, rinsed (see Tips, below)
1 piece fresh ginger, about 1 inch (2.5 cm), peeled and finely grated
10 dried jujubes (red dates)
2 tablespoons dried goji berries
Kosher salt, to taste
Ground white pepper, to taste (see Tips, below)

1 In a large stockpot over high heat, combine the pork bones with enough water to cover, approximately 1 gallon (3.8 L). Bring to a boil. Cook for 15 minutes. Remove the bones and rinse them thoroughly to remove any scum. Discard the water and wipe out the stockpot.
2 In the same stockpot over high heat, just cover the cleaned pork bones with fresh water. Add the ginger, jujubes and goji berries. Bring to a boil.
3 Reduce the heat to low and simmer the broth for about 3 hours, uncovered, until very flavorful and aromatic. Strain the broth into a clean pot and season with salt and pepper. Discard the bones and aromatics.
4 Use this broth immediately or let cool and refrigerate for up to 1 week or freeze for up to 2 months.

TIPS
► Ask your butcher for pork knuckles, trotters, leg, neck, or hip bones. Almost any bones will work with this recipe.

► Start with minimal amounts of salt and pepper and add more to taste. White pepper is strong and has a very distinct flavor.

Basic Sukiyaki Sauce

Of all the Asian hot pots, sukiyaki is the most popular in my family and one of the easiest to prepare. The ingredients are easy to find and the fact that it can be made ahead of time makes pulling the actual meal together something you can do in 20 minutes when you come home from work.

SKILL LEVEL: Easy
PREP TIME: 5 minutes
COOK TIME: 10 minutes
YIELD: 6 to 8 servings

INGREDIENTS

1 cup (240 ml) soy sauce
¼ cup (60 ml) sake
¼ cup (60 ml) mirin
¼ cup (50 g) sugar

1 In a small saucepan over medium-high heat, combine all the ingredients and bring to a boil.
2 Reduce the heat to low and simmer for about 5 minutes, whisking occasionally.
3 Transfer to a heatproof jar and let cool. Refrigerate until ready to use.
4 This sauce can be made ahead and refrigerated for up to 1 week or frozen for up to 1 month.

Ponzu Sauce

The delicate flavor of the yuzu citrus fruit is what makes this sauce so addictive (trust me; you'll want to put it on everything). Bottled yuzu juice can be found at Asian markets, but if you're lucky enough to find the fruit fresh, this is the place to use it. Yuzu is a difficult flavor to replicate, but if you can't find yuzu juice, a combination of fresh lemon and lime juices comes pretty close. I like a ponzu sauce that is more soy-sauce heavy, rather than too acidic, so I use a very high-quality, strong-tasting soy sauce here. Ponzu sauce is great with anything, but I prefer it with hot pots containing meat or seafood.

SKILL LEVEL: Easy
PREP TIME: 10 minutes
YIELD: Makes 1½ cups (360 ml)

INGREDIENTS

¾ cup (180 ml) soy sauce
6 tablespoons mirin
¼ cup (60 ml) yuzu juice (from 2 fresh yuzu or bottled; or the juice of 1 lemon and 1 lime)
2 tablespoons peeled, grated daikon radish
2 scallions, white part only, thinly sliced

1 In a small bowl, whisk together all the ingredients until blended.
2 This sauce can be refrigerated for up to 1 week

Chirizu Sauce

Yuzu, a Japanese citrus fruit, is the star of this bright, punchy sauce. You can buy good bottled yuzu juice, but if you're lucky enough to find the tangerine-size fruit fresh, take advantage of it. This sauce is similar to the traditional Ponzu Sauce on the facing page, but adds grated radish and ginger, plus the shichimi togarashi spice blend for a peppery kick. It's great for finishing fish because it adds a pleasant hit of acidity, which goes nicely with lean proteins. Serve a little bit in small bowls alongside your hot pot, as fish and vegetables only need a quick dip.

SKILL LEVEL: Easy
PREP TIME: 10 minutes
YIELD: Makes ¾ cup (180 ml)

INGREDIENTS
¼ cup (60 ml) yuzu juice (from 2 fresh yuzu or bottled; or the juice of 1 lemon and 1 lime)
¼ cup (60 ml) sake
3 tablespoons soy sauce
1 tablespoon mirin
2 tablespoons finely grated onion
1 piece fresh ginger, about 1 inch (2.5 cm), peeled and finely grated
1 tablespoon finely grated daikon radish
¼ teaspoon shichimi togarashi spice blend, or red pepper flakes

1 In a small bowl, stir together all the ingredients until blended.
2 This sauce can be made ahead and refrigerated for up to 1 week.

Chili-Cilantro-Lime Sauce

This is one of my friend Emily Lai's favorite sauces and her inspiration comes from Hainan, a small province in the southernmost part of China. It's typically served with Hainanese poached chicken rice, one of the region's most traditional and popular dishes. She told me there is a Thai version of this dish called Khao Man Gai, and in Vietnam, it's called Com Ga Hai Nam. She says this sauce goes well with anything as it has the right balance of spice, tartness and sweetness, along with herbaceous notes. Emily has even given a recipe for Hainanese poached chicken rice if you want to try to make it: "Poach a whole chicken in a water broth of ginger, cilantro and scallions, low and slow. Shock the cooked chicken in ice water. Slice or cut the chicken. Make rice using the poaching liquid. Serve the rice and chicken with the broth and two sauces. It's definitely a skill to make this, although it sounds simple. It's one of my favorite things to eat!"

SKILL LEVEL: Easy
PREP TIME: 5 minutes
YIELD: Makes ½ cup (120 ml)

INGREDIENTS
½ cup (8 g) loosely packed fresh cilantro leaves
¼ cup (60 g) sambal chili paste
¼ cup (60 ml) water
2 tablespoons fresh lime juice (from 1 lime)
Kosher salt, to taste

1 In a food processor, combine the cilantro, sambal chili paste, water and lime juice. Puree until smooth.
2 Season with salt.
3 This sauce can be made ahead and refrigerated for up to 2 days.

Sweet-and-Sour Layu Chili Sauce

I originally created this sauce as an accompaniment to my Vietnamese Oxtail Hot Pot (page 112), because so many Vietnamese dishes play with that hot, sweet-and-sour balance. My secret ingredient here is layu, a chili oil commonly used as a Japanese condiment to add spice to any dish. The mirin and hoisin sauce give this sauce its sweetness, the vinegar gives it that little bit of sour tang, and the layu and sriracha come in for a sneaky kick at the end. If you're a fiend for heat and are serving this with a mild dish, feel free to amp up the spice with more sriracha and layu.

SKILL LEVEL: Easy
PREP TIME: 5 minutes
YIELD: Makes ¾ cup (180 ml)

INGREDIENTS
¼ cup (60 ml) soy sauce
¼ cup (60 ml) mirin
2 tablespoons rice vinegar
1 tablespoon hoisin sauce
2 teaspoons sriracha
5 or 6 dashes layu, or chili oil, plus more to taste

1 In a small bowl, whisk together all the ingredients until smooth.
2 This sauce can be made ahead and refrigerated for up to 1 week.

Sesame Miso Sauce

The key to this rich, nutty sauce is to toast the sesame seeds beforehand. Pre-toasted sesame seeds are fine in a pinch, but I suggest toasting them a little further to enhance the flavor. The final swirl of sesame oil also adds to the bold sesame flavor. I like to keep a jar of this sauce in the refrigerator because you can serve it with almost anything — as a sauce for meats and vegetables fresh out of the hot pot, as a salad dressing, or as a dip for crudités.

SKILL LEVEL: Easy
PREP TIME: 10 minutes
COOK TIME: 10 minutes
YIELD: Makes 1½ cups (360 ml)

INGREDIENTS

½ cup (70 g) white sesame seeds
½ cup (130 g) white miso paste
2 tablespoons sugar
1 tablespoon soy sauce
1 tablespoon mirin
2 teaspoons rice vinegar
2 large garlic cloves, crushed
¾ cup (180 ml) water, plus more if needed
1 tablespoon toasted sesame oil

1 In a small dry skillet over low heat, toast the sesame seeds for about 10 minutes, until fragrant and golden brown, constantly stirring or swirling the seeds in the pan as they cook. Let cool, then transfer to a mortar with a pestle or clean coffee grinder. Crush the toasted sesame seeds into a fine powder (see Tip, below).
2 In a blender, combine the miso, sugar, soy sauce, mirin, vinegar, garlic, water and the ground sesame seeds. Puree until smooth. The sauce should have the consistency of a salad dressing. Add more water, if needed.
3 Scrape the sauce into a small bowl and stir in the sesame oil before serving.
4 This sauce can be made ahead and refrigerated for up to 1 week.

TIP If you use a coffee grinder, take care not to overprocess the seeds or you'll end up with sesame paste. Stop grinding before the seeds start to release oil so that the powder doesn't clump.

Steamed Japanese Rice

Japanese rice is short grain, higher in starch than long-grain rice, which gives it that signature sticky consistency. It comes in brown varieties, too, and there is also a delicious in-between rice called haiga. When looking at the different types, the higher quality rice you purchase, the better it will taste. If you are at an Asian or a Japanese market, you'll see a range of rices to choose from, so try a few different brands to find your favorite.

SKILL LEVEL: Easy
PREP TIME: 10 minutes
COOK TIME: 1 hour 15 minutes
YIELD: 4 to 6 servings

INGREDIENTS

2 cups (400 g) white or brown Japanese short-grain rice

1 Place the rice in a fine-mesh sieve. Gently rinse the rice with cold water and rub the grains together in your palms to loosen the starches, releasing the milky water. Repeat 4 to 6 times until the water runs clear.
2 Put the rice in a 4-quart (3.8 L) saucepan or 4- to 6-cup (960 ml to 1.4 L) rice cooker and pat it down into an even layer. Cover the rice with enough water so when the tip of your thumb touches the surface of the rice, the water rises to your knuckle — about 1 inch (2.5 cm). Let the rice soak in the water for about 15 minutes. (This makes for a fluffier final product, especially if your rice is not super fresh and a tad dried out.)
3 If using a rice cooker, follow the manufacturer's instructions (see Tip, below). If using a saucepan, place the pan of rice and water from Step 2 over high heat and bring to a boil.
4 Reduce the heat to low, cover the pan and simmer until just tender, about 30 minutes for white rice and about 40 minutes for brown rice.
5 Remove the saucepan from the heat and let the rice steam, covered, for about 15 minutes. Fluff with a fork and serve.

TIP You may find my method for cooking rice in this recipe a bit unusual, but I promise it works — every time. We don't measure the cooking water with a cup, we measure it with our thumb. Regardless of how much rice you use or whether or not you cook your rice in a saucepan or rice cooker, this trick works!

Roasted Nori Seaweed

These days you can find roasted and flavored nori seaweed in grocery stores, coffee shops — even vending machines. While I appreciate the convenience of pre-roasted nori seaweed, I prefer to roast my own because I feel like some of the varieties out there are too oily or don't stay crisp. If you purchase a package of big sheets of unroasted seaweed for sushi, you can roast them over an open gas flame in seconds, which results in much fresher, crispier and toastier sheets. Plus, you can make many more for the cost. I promise you'll never go back to those instant packs. My kids like to snack on these plain, as if they are potato chips, but they can also be rolled up with rice, slipped into a bowl of ramen, or wrapped up like sushi hand rolls with fresh fish and julienned vegetables. One thing to note — you do need a gas range to make these!

SKILL LEVEL: Easy
PREP TIME: 2 minutes
COOK TIME: 5 minutes
YIELD: Makes about 40 small squares

INGREDIENTS

10 sheets nori seaweed, each approximately 8 x 8 inches (20 x 20 cm)
Cooking spray, preferably sesame or coconut oil
Fine sea salt, for sprinkling

1 Line a plate with paper towels and set aside.

2 Spray both sides of each seaweed sheet with cooking spray or use a paper towel to apply a thin coat of oil on each side.

3 Over a low flame on a gas stovetop, using tongs, gently waft the seaweed back and forth on both sides until it crisps up, about 5 seconds. Be careful not to hold the seaweed directly over the flame for too long or it will catch fire. Transfer the roasted seaweed to the prepared plate and sprinkle with salt. Repeat with the remaining seaweed.

4 Transfer the roasted nori to a cutting board and lay 5 sheets on top of each other. Using a chef's knife or kitchen shears, cut the stack into 4 small squares. Repeat with the remaining 5 sheets of roasted nori.

5 Store in an airtight container or resealable plastic bag for up to 3 days.

Chicken
Hot Pots

HOT TIP

Freeze the chicken up to
4 hours so it is firm and
easier to slice, or purchase
sukiyaki or shabu-shabu
chicken at Asian markets
or ask your butcher
to thinly slice it.

Chicken Sukiyaki

SKILL LEVEL: Moderate
PREP TIME: 15 minutes
COOK TIME: 15 minutes
YIELD: 4 to 6 servings
PREPARATION: At the table

TO MAKE IN ADVANCE

Basic Sukiyaki Sauce (page 36)
Sesame Miso Sauce (page 38)

INGREDIENTS

1 pound (454 g) chicken breasts, very thinly sliced (see Hot Tip)

5 ounces (140 g) wood ear or fresh shiitake mushrooms, cleaned

3 baby bok choy, quartered lengthwise

1 bunch shungiku chrysanthemum leaves or watercress, stemmed

1 large carrot, shaved into thin ribbons or cut into flower shapes

½ medium sweet onion, thinly sliced

½ small satsumaimo (Japanese sweet potato) or regular sweet potato, peeled and very thinly sliced on a mandoline

1 block firm tofu, 14 ounces (400 g) drained and cut into 1-inch (2.5 cm) cubes

4–6 portions packaged white shirataki noodles, drained

2 tablespoons vegetable oil, divided

2 large garlic cloves, minced, divided

½ cup (120 ml) Basic Sukiyaki Sauce, divided, plus more as needed

Toasted sesame seeds, for garnishing

Sesame Miso Sauce, for serving

One of our family favorites, this sukiyaki came about when my in-laws were visiting, and I wanted to show them how to make it. They were huge fans of the easy preparation and liked trying new vegetables they had never heard of; however, you don't need to worry if you can't get your hands on those specialty ingredients. Almost any leftover vegetable in your fridge will work here. Broccoli? Yes! Sliced bell peppers? Totally. My in-laws also could not get enough of the creamy, nutty sesame miso sauce. The savory sauce is perfect for dunking the tender, delicately seasoned chicken and vegetables. This hot pot is not super filling, so the shirataki noodles cooked in the remaining sukiyaki sauce perfectly round out the meal. But if you are protein lovers, add more chicken. In-law success!

1 Arrange the chicken, vegetables, tofu and noodles on platters. Place the platters on the table around the hot pot.

2 In a 4-quart (3.8 L) hot pot or large saucepan over medium-high heat (about 425°F, or 220°C, in an electric hot pot), heat 1 tablespoon of the vegetable oil until shimmering. Add half the garlic. Cook for about 1 minute, stirring, until fragrant.

3 Add half the vegetables and tofu to the pot. Cook for about 2 minutes, stirring occasionally, until the vegetables begin to soften.

4 Arrange half the sliced chicken on top of the vegetables and drizzle with ¼ cup (60 ml) of the sukiyaki sauce. Reduce the heat to medium. Cook for about 1 minute, until the chicken begins to turn white. Flip the chicken and cook for 1 minute more.

5 Fold the chicken into the vegetables and tofu until evenly coated with the sauce. Continue to cook until the chicken is cooked through and the vegetables are just tender, about 1 minute more. If food starts to stick to the bottom of the hot pot, reduce the heat and add a little water to cool it down.

6 Transfer the chicken sukiyaki to individual plates and garnish with sesame seeds. Serve with the sesame miso sauce.

7 Repeat the process with the remaining 1 tablespoon vegetable oil, garlic clove, vegetables, tofu, chicken and ¼ cup (60 ml) sukiyaki sauce.

8 When the vegetables, tofu and chicken have been eaten and you are left with just the sauce in the bottom of the hot pot, add the shirataki noodles. Cook for 2 to 3 minutes, stirring, until heated through and coated with the sauce, adding more sauce, if needed. Serve the noodles as the shime (end-of-meal course).

Chanko Nabe Sumo Hot Pot

The name of this hearty recipe from my friend Kiko can be translated as "parent and child," referring to the close bond between sumo wrestlers, and their communal eating habits. Traditionally, this was a dish that teammates would make for each other to help gain weight: it's packed with lean proteins including chicken, pork and shrimp, to give sumo wrestlers strength and energy for competing — but if you prefer to use just one or two of these proteins, it will be equally delicious. I think the ground chicken meatballs are the best part of this hot pot; they are flavored with dried shiitake, instead of fresh, for added umami and a deeper mushroom flavor. The tender meatballs float in the dashi-based broth like plump dumplings. While you might not be feeding a team of sumo wrestlers, I promise this hot pot will be equally successful at satisfying your family and friends.

SKILL LEVEL: Moderate
PREP TIME: 40 minutes
COOK TIME: 20 minutes, plus 1 hour soaking time
YIELD: 4 to 6 servings
PREPARATION: Stovetop

TO MAKE IN ADVANCE

Basic Dashi Stock (page 26)
Steamed Japanese Rice (page 38)

INGREDIENTS

FOR THE MEATBALLS
½ cup (60 g) cornstarch
1 pound (450 g) ground chicken (dark meat only)
2 scallions, white and light green parts only, thinly sliced
2 dried shiitake mushrooms, soaked in warm water for 1 hour, drained and finely chopped
½ medium Vidalia onion, finely chopped
1 piece fresh ginger, about 1 inch (2.5 cm), peeled and finely grated
1 teaspoon sake
1 teaspoon sugar
1 teaspoon kosher salt
1/8 teaspoon freshly ground black pepper

FOR THE HOT POT
2 quarts (1.9 L) Basic Dashi Stock, or dashi made with an instant mix
½ cup (120 ml) soy sauce
½ cup (120 ml) sake
1 teaspoon sugar
1 teaspoon kosher salt
8 ounces (220 g) pork loin, very thinly sliced (see Hot Tip)
6–8 large shrimp, about 8 ounces (220 g), shelled, tails on and deveined
4 rectangular pieces of aburaage fried tofu
4–6 portions packaged white shirataki noodles, drained
6 fresh shiitake mushrooms, cleaned and stemmed
5 ounces (140 g) forest nameko mushrooms, or buna-shimeji mushrooms, or enoki mushrooms, cleaned, trimmed and torn into large pieces
4 large scallions, white and light green parts only, cut diagonally into 3-inch (7.5 cm) lengths
1 medium sweet onion, cut into ¼-inch (5 mm)-thick rings
¼ head Napa cabbage, cored and thick white parts cut into bite-size pieces
Steamed Japanese Rice, for serving

HOT TIP

Freeze the pork up to 4 hours so it is firm and easier to slice or purchase sukiyaki or shabu-shabu pork at Asian markets or ask your butcher to thinly slice it.

1. To make the meatballs: Bring a large pot of water to a boil over high heat. Line a plate with paper towels and set aside. Spread the cornstarch in a shallow bowl.

2. In a large bowl, mix together all the remaining meatball ingredients. (Be careful not to overmix or the meatballs will be dense.) Wet your hands with a little water and form the mixture into ping-pong–size balls. You should have about 12 meatballs. Dredge the meatballs in the cornstarch and transfer to a plate.

3. Gently drop the meatballs into the boiling water and cook until they rise to the surface and are partially cooked through, about 2 minutes. Using a slotted spoon, transfer the parboiled meatballs to the paper towel–lined plate to drain.

4. To make the hot pot: Heat a 4-quart (3.8 L) hot pot or large saucepan over medium-high heat (about 425°F, or 220°C, in an electric pot). Add the dashi, soy sauce, sake, sugar and salt. Bring to a boil.

5. Add the sliced pork, shrimp, aburaage, noodles, vegetables and parboiled meatballs. Cover the pot and reduce the heat to low. Simmer for about 5 minutes, until the pork, shrimp and meatballs are just cooked through and the vegetables are tender.

6. Ladle into shallow bowls and serve.

7. After the meat, tofu, noodles and vegetables have been eaten, add the steamed rice to the remaining broth and let it soak up the liquid, like a risotto, stirring occasionally, until most of the broth has been absorbed. Serve the porridge as the shime (end-of-meal course).

SKILL LEVEL: Moderate
PREP TIME: 30 minutes, plus 2 hours marinating time
COOK TIME: 30 minutes
YIELD: 4 to 6 servings
PREPARATION: Stovetop

TO MAKE IN ADVANCE

Chicken Stock (page 26)
Steamed Japanese Rice (page 38)

INGREDIENTS

1½ pounds (680 g) boneless skinless chicken thighs, cut into bite-size pieces
4 ounces (120 g) fresh shiitake mushrooms, cleaned and stemmed
3 ounces (85 g) enoki mushrooms, cleaned and trimmed
Kosher salt, to taste
Freshly ground black pepper, to taste
4 tablespoons shio koji, divided
2 tablespoons olive oil, divided
2 tablespoons sesame oil
5 cups (1.2 L) Chicken Stock, or store-bought low-sodium chicken broth
¼ cup (60 ml) sake
2 tablespoons soy sauce
2 medium carrots, sliced 1 inch (2.5 cm) thick on the diagonal, or cut into flower shapes
2 large scallions, white and light green parts only, cut into 1½-inch (3.5 cm) pieces
¼ head Napa cabbage, cored and the thick white parts cut into bite-size pieces
1 bunch shungiku chrysanthemum leaves, or watercress, stemmed
Steamed Japanese Rice, for serving

Shio Koji Chicken Hot Pot with Vegetables

This colorful hot pot has a light broth highlighted by the shio koji, soy sauce and sake. Shio koji is an umami-rich condiment made from salt (shio) and rice that is fermented with koji, the edible fungus used to make miso and sake. By marinating both the chicken and the mushrooms in shio koji, these ingredients then season the broth when added to the hot pot. You can find shio koji at most Japanese markets and online.

1 Place the chicken into a medium bowl and the mushrooms into a separate medium bowl. Season each with the salt and pepper.

2 Add 3 tablespoons of the shio koji to the chicken and the remaining 1 tablespoon to the mushrooms. Toss each to coat. Cover each bowl with plastic wrap and refrigerate for 2 hours.

3 In a medium skillet over medium heat, heat 1 tablespoon of the olive oil. Add half the chicken to the skillet. Cook for 4 to 5 minutes, stirring occasionally, until browned, but not fully cooked. Transfer to a clean bowl and repeat with the remaining 1 tablespoon olive oil and chicken. Wipe out the skillet.

4 Return the skillet to medium heat and heat the sesame oil. Add the mushrooms. Cook for 4 to 5 minutes, stirring occasionally, until tender.

5 Heat a 4-quart (3.8 L) hot pot or large saucepan over medium-high heat (about 425°F, or 220°C, in an electric pot). Add the chicken stock, sake and soy sauce. Bring to a boil.

6 Add the carrots, scallions, cabbage and the chicken and its juices. Cover the pot and reduce the heat to low. Simmer for about 15 minutes, until the vegetables are just tender and the chicken is cooked through. Add the chrysanthemum leaves and the mushrooms.

7 Serve in shallow bowls with the steamed rice on the side.

Chicken Hot Pot with Soy Milk

SKILL LEVEL: Easy
PREP TIME: 15 minutes
COOK TIME: 30 minutes
YIELD: 4 to 6 servings
PREPARATION: Stovetop

TO MAKE IN ADVANCE

Soy Milk Broth (page 29)
Steamed Japanese Rice (page 38)

INGREDIENTS

1 tablespoon bacon fat, or vegetable oil
1 piece fresh ginger, about 1½ inches (3.5 cm), peeled and finely grated
2 large garlic cloves, peeled and minced
1½ pounds (680 g) ground chicken, preferably dark meat
Kosher salt, to taste
Freshly ground black pepper, to taste
5 cups (1.2 L) Soy Milk Broth
½ small kabocha pumpkin, seeded and cut into bite-size pieces
¼ head Napa cabbage, cored and thick white parts cut into bite-size pieces
1 tablespoon sesame oil
2–3 large bok choy, sliced lengthwise
1 cup (100 g) bean sprouts
2–3 large eggs, medium-boiled and sliced in half
Steamed Japanese Rice, for serving
Chili threads, for garnish
Shichimi togarashi spice blend, or red pepper flakes, to taste
Chili oil, to taste

This is one of those Japanese comfort foods that's perfect for a cold winter's day when you just want to stay at home and have something that soothes the soul. The sweetness of the soy milk and miso combine perfectly with the ground chicken and vegetables. Unlike other thick-skinned squash, kabocha does not need to be peeled, so this dish can be pulled together quickly. Also, if you don't have time to make fresh dashi or chicken stock, use store-bought versions.

1 In a 4-quart (3.8 L) hot pot or large saucepan over medium-high heat (about 425°F, or 220°C, in an electric hot pot), heat the bacon fat. Add the ginger and garlic. Cook for about 1 minute, stirring, until fragrant.

2 Add the ground chicken. Season with salt and pepper. Cook for about 5 minutes, breaking up the chicken with a spoon, until just cooked through. Remove from heat and set aside in a separate bowl.

3 Put the soy milk broth into the same saucepan, turn the heat to high and bring to a boil.

4 Add the kabocha. Reduce the heat to low, cover the pot and simmer for about 15 minutes, until the kabocha is just tender.

5 Add the cabbage. Cover the pot and simmer for 5 minutes more.

6 While the cabbage is cooking, put the sesame oil into a separate saucepan over medium-high heat. Add the bok choy and sauté for 2 minutes on each side until cooked through. Remove from the heat and set aside.

7 Divide the steamed rice among serving bowls. Ladle the soup over the top of each bowl with equal portions of cabbage and kabocha. Spoon a mound of the ground chicken from Step 2, a handful of bean sprouts, half a medium-boiled egg and a piece of bok choy from Step 6 onto the soup. Garnish with the chili threads, sprinkle with shichimi togarashi and chili oil if desired

Chicken and Egg Hot Pot with Ramen

SKILL LEVEL: Moderate
PREP TIME: 30 minutes, plus 1 hour marinating time
COOK TIME: 20 minutes
YIELD: 4 to 6 servings
PREPARATION: Stovetop

TO MAKE IN ADVANCE

Sesame Miso Broth, spicy (page 32)
Steamed Japanese Rice (page 38)

INGREDIENTS

FOR THE TERIYAKI SAUCE

1 cup (240 ml) soy sauce
1 cup (200 g) sugar
1 piece fresh ginger, about 1½ inches (3.5 cm), peeled and finely grated
2 large garlic cloves, minced
½ cup (120 ml) mirin

FOR THE HOT POT

1½ pounds (680 g) boneless skinless chicken thighs, cut into bite-size pieces
4 cups (960 ml) Sesame Miso Broth, spicy
5 ounces (140 g) cremini mushrooms, cleaned, trimmed and sliced lengthwise, or shiitake, stemmed
3 large bok choy, sliced lengthwise
1 package kamaboko fish cake, about 6 oz (170 g), sliced thinly
4 rectangular pieces aburaage fried tofu
8 oz (220 g) uncooked, fresh ramen noodles
4–6 large eggs
Steamed Japanese Rice, for serving
Red pepper flakes, for garnish

This dish reminds me of my childhood when we would eat oyakodon, a traditional Japanese comfort food made with chicken and eggs, and laden with a dashi and soy sauce–based sauce soaked up by the fluffy steamed rice scooped on top. In this recipe, the combination of the spicy sesame miso broth and marinated chicken teriyaki offers similar flavors to that umami-filled dish my siblings and I craved growing up. This is super kid-friendly, very filling and one of my family's favorite Sunday-night hot pots.

1 To make the teriyaki sauce: In a medium saucepan over high heat, combine the soy sauce, sugar, ginger and garlic. Bring to a boil. As soon as it boils, reduce the heat to low and whisk in the mirin. Remove from the heat. (This makes more than you will need for this recipe. Refrigerate the leftover sauce for up to 2 weeks and use as a marinade for salmon, beef, chicken or vegetables.)

2 To make the hot pot: In a small bowl, toss the chicken thighs with ¼ cup (60 ml) of the teriyaki sauce. Cover and refrigerate for 1 hour.

3 Heat a 4-quart (3.8 L) hot pot or large saucepan over medium-high heat (about 425°F, or 220°C, in an electric hot pot). Add the spicy sesame miso broth. Bring to a boil.

4 Add the chicken to the hot pot. Cover the pot and cook for about 10 minutes, until the chicken is almost done.

5 Add the vegetables, fish cake, aburaage and ramen to the broth with the chicken, arranging them in an appealing way. Cook for 5 minutes until the vegetables are tender and the fish cake and tofu are heated through.

6 Crack the eggs into the hot pot, scattering them throughout. Cover the pot and cook the eggs until the whites are just set and the yolks are still runny, about 3 minutes — the chicken should be fully cooked at this point.

7 Transfer to shallow bowls and serve with the steamed rice on the side. Garnish with the red pepper flakes.

Chicken and Duck Hot Pot

This light, clean broth really lets the flavor of the duck shine. Before gently simmering in the broth, the duck is cooked low and slow, keeping the meat juicy and tender — this also helps the fat render out and makes the skin extra crispy. The cooking process is simple, but it does require some patience. Start with the duck, skin side down, in a cold pan while you slowly turn up the heat. If you start with a hot pan or turn up the heat before the fat starts to render, a crust will form on the duck and you'll be left with a thick, chewy piece of duck skin. Don't discard the leftover duck fat in the skillet — it is repurposed for cooking the shallots, ginger and garlic (and also adding more duck flavor to the soup). The Sweet-and-Sour Layu Chili Sauce is not optional here; it makes the perfect accompaniment to the poultry and the duck.

HOT TIP

Shoyu koji, also called soy sauce koji, is a savory condiment made of fermented rice and soy sauce, sold at Asian markets and online. If you can't find it, season the chicken with salt and add 1 additional tablespoon of soy sauce to the dashi with the sake and mirin.

SKILL LEVEL: Moderate
PREP TIME: 30 minutes, plus 2 hours marinating time
COOK TIME: 40 minutes
YIELD: 4 to 6 servings
PREPARATION: Stovetop

TO MAKE IN ADVANCE

Basic Dashi Stock (page 26)
Sweet-and-Sour Layu Chili Sauce (page 37)
Steamed Japanese Rice (page 38)

INGREDIENTS

1½ pounds (680 g) boneless skinless chicken thighs, cut into bite-size pieces
1 tablespoon shoyu koji (see Hot Tip)
2 skin-on duck breasts, each about 10 ounces (300 g)
Kosher salt, to taste
Freshly ground black pepper, to taste
1 medium shallot, thinly sliced
1 piece fresh ginger, about 1 inch (2.5 cm), peeled and finely grated
2 large garlic cloves, minced
2 quarts (1.9 L) Basic Dashi Stock, or dashi made with an instant mix
¼ cup (60 ml) sake
¼ cup (60 ml) mirin
1 tablespoon soy sauce
2 cups (180 g) packed very thinly sliced red cabbage
5 ounces (140 g) king trumpet mushrooms, or brown cremini mushrooms, cleaned, trimmed and sliced lengthwise
1 large carrot, shaved into thin ribbons with a vegetable peeler
1 block medium-firm tofu, 14 ounces (400 g), drained and cut into 1-inch (2.5 cm) cubes
4–6 portions packaged white shirataki noodles, drained
Steamed Japanese Rice, for serving
Sweet-and-Sour Layu Chili Sauce, for serving

1 In a small bowl, toss the chicken thighs with the shoyu koji. Cover and refrigerate for at least 2 hours. Pat the duck breasts dry with paper towels and season with salt and pepper.

2 In a cold, medium nonstick skillet, place the duck skin side down. Place the skillet over medium-low heat and cook, without turning until the duck fat has rendered and the skin is beginning to brown, about 15 minutes. You should hear a low sizzle. If the fat starts to splatter, lower the heat.

3 Increase the heat to high and cook for 2 to 3 minutes more, until the skin is golden and caramelized. Transfer the duck to a cutting board and let rest for 10 minutes. Slice the breasts about ½ inch (1 cm) thick. The duck should still be slightly raw. Pour the duck fat into a small heatproof bowl and reserve.

4 In a 4-quart (3.8 L) hot pot or large saucepan over medium heat (about 400°F, or 200°C, in an electric pot), heat 2 tablespoons of the reserved duck fat. Add the shallot, ginger and garlic. Cook for about 5 minutes, stirring occasionally, until the shallot is translucent.

5 Add the dashi, sake, mirin and soy sauce to the hot pot and bring to a boil. Add the marinated chicken. Cover the pot, reduce the heat to low and simmer for 5 minutes.

6 Add the vegetables, tofu and noodles. Cover the pot and cook for 5 minutes more.

7 Lay the sliced duck over the top of the vegetables. Cook, covered, for about 2 minutes more, until the chicken is cooked through, the vegetables are tender and the duck is slightly pink.

8 Ladle into shallow bowls and serve with the steamed rice on the side and the layu chili sauce for dipping.

Beef Hot Pots

Rib Eye Shabu-Shabu

SKILL LEVEL: Moderate
PREP TIME: 30 minutes
COOK TIME: 15 minutes
YIELD: 4 to 6 servings
PREPARATION: At the table

TO MAKE IN ADVANCE

Basic Shabu-Shabu Broth (page 29)
Sesame Miso Sauce (page 38)

INGREDIENTS

1½ pounds (680 g) Rib Eye beef, very thinly sliced (see Hot Tips)

1 bunch shungiku chrysanthemum leaves, or watercress, stemmed

3 ounces (85 g) buna-shimeji mushrooms or enoki mushrooms, cleaned and trimmed, or shiitake mushrooms, stemmed

¼ head Napa cabbage, cored and thick white parts cut into bite-size pieces

1 block firm tofu, 14 ounces (400 g), drained and cut into 1-inch (2.5 cm) cubes

4–6 portions packaged white shirataki noodles, drained

2 quarts (1.9 L) Basic Shabu-Shabu Broth (see Hot Tips)

1 green onion, sliced into 2-inch (5 cm) pieces

Sesame Miso Sauce, for serving

The simplicity of shabu-shabu allows the quality of the ingredients to shine through — and this recipe is a classic example of the dish. It's important to have vegetables that are quick to cook, so if you add any extra ingredients like root vegetables, make sure they are sliced very thinly. This is a perfect recipe to make when you can visit a farmers' market and have your pick of what's in season. Splurge on a good rib eye, as the meat is the hero here, and the sesame miso sauce pretty much makes everything better.

1 Arrange the beef, vegetables, tofu and noodles on platters. Place the platters on the table around the hot pot.

2 Heat a 4-quart (3.8 L) hot pot or large saucepan over medium-high heat (about 425°F, or 220°C, in an electric hot pot). Add the shabu-shabu broth and green onion and bring to a boil.

3 Let everyone add their own meat, vegetables and tofu and noodles, swishing back and forth in the hot broth until the vegetables are tender and the meat is still slightly pink, 1 to 2 minutes. As food is added, adjust the heat to maintain a low boil. Serve with the sesame miso sauce for dipping.

HOT TIPS

▶ Freeze the beef up to 4 hours so it is firm and easier to slice or purchase sukiyaki or shabu-shabu beef at Asian markets or ask your butcher to thinly slice it.

▶ This recipe is easy to scale up or down. Just make sure your hot pot is filled about halfway with broth. If the liquid reduces over time, add more.

Wagyu Beef Sukiyaki

SKILL LEVEL: Easy
PREP TIME: 30 minutes
COOK TIME: 20 minutes
YIELD: 4 to 6 servings
PREPARATION: At the table

TO MAKE IN ADVANCE

Basic Sukiyaki Sauce (page 36)

INGREDIENTS

1½ pounds (680 g) wagyu beef, or Rib Eye or Angus beef, very thinly sliced (see Hot Tip)

5 ounces (140 g) fresh shiitake mushrooms, cleaned, trimmed and sliced

1 bunch watercress, stemmed

1 large carrot, shaved into thin ribbons with a vegetable peeler

1 cup (100 g) sugar snap peas, trimmed

1 block extra-firm tofu, 14 ounces (400 g), drained and cut into 1-inch (2.5 cm) cubes

4–6 servings frozen, cooked udon noodles, thawed

2 pieces beef suet, about 1 inch (2.5 cm) each, or 2 tablespoons bacon fat or vegetable oil)

½ medium sweet onion, thinly sliced, divided

½ cup (120 ml) Basic Sukiyaki Sauce, divided, plus more as needed

Toasted white sesame seeds, for garnish

4–6 large eggs, lightly beaten (preferably pasteurized, as they will be eaten raw), optional

I like the ease of this dish — once the sukiyaki sauce is made, it is an incredibly simple meal you can make with any protein and vegetables you have on hand. Traditional sukiyaki is served with a lightly beaten egg that you dip the cooked beef and vegetables into before eating. This gives the food a silky, luxurious texture that's surprisingly addictive. I recommend serving this with my Simple Salad with Sesame Soy Dressing (page 118).

1. Arrange the beef, mushrooms, watercress, carrot, peas, tofu and noodles on platters. Place the platters on the table around the hot pot.

2. In a 4-quart (3.8 L) hot pot or large saucepan over medium-high heat (about 425°F, or 220°C, in an electric hot pot), melt 1 piece of suet until it is rendered. You may have a bit of cartilage left over, but you can keep it in the pot. Add half the onion. Cook for about 5 minutes, stirring occasionally, until translucent.

3. Add half the vegetables and tofu to the pot. Cook for about 2 minutes, stirring, until the vegetables begin to soften.

4. Arrange half the sliced beef on top of the vegetables. Drizzle with ¼ cup (60 ml) of the sukiyaki sauce. Reduce the heat to medium and cook for about 1 minute, until the beef begins to turn brown. Flip the beef and cook for 1 minute more.

5. Fold the beef into the vegetables and tofu until evenly coated with the sauce. Cook until the beef is tender and almost cooked through, about 1 minute more. If food starts to stick to the bottom of the pot, reduce the heat and add a little water to cool it down.

6. Transfer the beef sukiyaki to plates and garnish with sesame seeds. Serve with individual bowls of lightly beaten egg for dipping.

7. Repeat the process with the remaining suet, onion, vegetables, tofu, beef and ¼ cup (60 ml) sukiyaki sauce.

8. When the vegetables, tofu and beef have been eaten and you are left with just the sauce in the bottom of the hot pot, add the udon noodles. Cook for 2 to 3 minutes, stirring, until heated through and coated with sauce, adding more sauce, if needed. Serve the noodles as the shime (end-of-meal course).

HOT TIP

Freeze the pork up to 4 hours so it is firm and easier to slice or purchase sukiyaki or shabu-shabu pork at Asian markets or ask your butcher to thinly slice it.

Slow-Cooked Beef Brisket with Tomato Broth

SKILL LEVEL: Moderate
PREP TIME: 20 minutes
COOK TIME: 6 hours 30 minutes
YIELD: 4 to 6 servings
PREPARATION: Stovetop

TO MAKE IN ADVANCE

Tomato Broth (page 32)

INGREDIENTS

2 pounds (900 g) beef brisket
Kosher salt, to taste
Freshly ground black pepper, to taste
1 tablespoon olive oil
2 quarts (1.9 L) Tomato Broth (see Hot Tip)
1 large carrot, shaved into thin ribbons with a vegetable peeler
1 small can bamboo shoots, about 8 ounces (220 g), drained and sliced
1 leek, washed and sliced on the diagonal, white part only
1 bunch shungiku chrysanthemum leaves, or watercress, stemmed
5 ounces (140 g) king trumpet mushrooms, or brown cremini mushrooms, cleaned, trimmed and sliced lengthwise
½ small satsumaimo sweet potato; or any other variety of sweet potato, peeled and thinly sliced
1 block extra-firm tofu, 14 ounces (400g), drained, cut in half lengthwise and sliced into 1-inch (2.5 cm) strips
1 egg per person

This slow-cooked brisket is an homage to my mother-in-law, Clara, who makes the most tender, flavorful brisket for Passover. Although mine doesn't really compare to hers, my husband says it's not half bad — so I'll take that! Brisket is perfect for slow cooking because all its connective tissues break down and gelatinize over time. What this means is, if you are patient, it's one of the juiciest and most succulent cuts of beef you can get. Whatever you do, don't trim off the fat, as that is what traps in the moisture so you aren't left with a dry piece of meat. You can trim off the fat when you slice it later, but I think it's delicious just the way it is. I like to add an extra ladle of broth to everyone's bowls, along with a spoon, for a nice bowl of soup with meaty bits of goodness at the end.

1 Season the brisket with the salt and pepper.

2 Heat the olive oil in a large skillet over medium-high heat. Sear the meat in the skillet on all sides until browned, about 6 minutes per side. Transfer to a cutting board.

3 Heat a 4-quart (3.8 L) hot pot or large saucepan over medium-high heat (about 425°F, or 220°C, in an electric pot). Add the tomato broth and bring to a boil.

4 Add the brisket to the broth, fat side down. Cover the pot, reduce the heat to low and simmer for about 6 hours until tender and a fork can easily pierce the brisket. Remove the brisket from the pot and slice it ¼ inch (5 mm) thick.

5 Add the vegetables, tofu and sliced meat to the broth, arranging in an appealing way. Crack the eggs into the hot pot, scattering them throughout. Cover the pot and cook the eggs until the whites are just set and the yolks are still runny, about 3 minutes.

6 Ladle into shallow bowls and serve.

HOT TIP

This recipe is easy to scale up or down. Just make sure your hot pot is filled about halfway with broth. If the liquid reduces over time, add more.

Meat Lover's Macanese Hot Pot

SKILL LEVEL: Moderate
PREP TIME: 20 minutes
COOK TIME: 20 minutes
YIELD: 6 to 8 servings
PREPARATION: At the table

TO MAKE IN ADVANCE

Macanese Broth (page 35)
Chili-Cilantro-Lime Sauce (page 37)

INGREDIENTS

2 ounces (55 g) dried harusame cellophane noodles
Boiling water, to soften the noodles
8 ounces (220 g) wagyu, rib eye, or Angus beef, very thinly sliced (see Hot Tips)
8 ounces (220 g) pork loin, very thinly sliced (see Hot Tips)
8 ounces (220 g) boneless, skinless chicken breast, very thinly sliced (see Hot Tips)
5 ounces (140 g) forest nameko mushrooms, or buna-shimeji or enoki mushrooms, cleaned, trimmed and torn into small bunches
2 cups (60 g) packed baby spinach
1 block firm tofu, 14 ounces (400 g), drained and cut into 1-inch (2.5 cm) cubes
2 quarts (1.9 L) Macanese Broth (see Hot Tips)
2 ears fresh corn, shucked and cut into 2-inch (5 cm) pieces
Lime wedges, for garnish
Fresh cilantro leaves, for garnish
Thinly sliced Fresno peppers, or jalapeño peppers, for garnish
Tahini, for serving
Chili-Cilantro-Lime Sauce, for serving

This hot pot was created by my friend Emily Lai and inspired by her family and their love of hot pots. Although she is Malaysian, this hot pot, originating in Macau, was a staple in her house growing up. She recalls that whenever her parents or aunts and uncles threw a party, it was always a hot pot party. It was not only an easy way for them to feed the whole family, but it also allowed all the young cousins to help with the "cooking," as they dipped their food into the bubbling broth and served themselves. Emily's family held their hot pot parties late into the evening — cooking, eating, drinking, chatting, breaking for a bit and then repeating.

1 Place the dried noodles in a large heatproof bowl and cover with boiling water. Let sit for about 10 minutes, until softened. Rinse under cold water, drain well and cut in half.

2 Arrange the beef, pork, chicken, mushrooms, spinach, tofu and noodles on platters. Place the platters on the table around the hot pot.

3 Heat a 4-quart (3.8 L) hot pot or large saucepan over medium-high heat (about 425°F, or 220°C, in an electric pot). Add the Macanese broth and corn and bring to a boil.

4 Let everyone add their own meat (beef, pork, or chicken), vegetables, tofu and noodles, swishing back and forth in the hot broth until tender and cooked through, 1 to 2 minutes. As food is added, adjust the heat to maintain a low boil.

5 Serve with the lime wedges, cilantro, Fresno peppers, tahini and the chili-cilantro-lime sauce, as desired.

HOT TIPS

► Freeze the meat up to 4 hours until it is firm and easier to slice or purchase sukiyaki or shabu-shabu meat at Asian markets or ask your butcher to thinly slice it.

► This recipe is easy to scale up or down. Just make sure your hot pot is filled about halfway with broth. If the liquid reduces over time, add more.

Beef Curry Hot Pot

TO MAKE IN ADVANCE

Japanese Curry Broth (page 30)
Steamed Japanese Rice (page 38)

INGREDIENTS

1½ pounds (680 g) cubed beef stew
  meat (chuck is best)
Kosher salt, to taste
Freshly ground black pepper, to
  taste
All-purpose flour, for dusting
1 tablespoon olive oil, plus more as
  needed
2 quarts (1.9 L) Japanese Curry Broth
8–10 small potatoes, about 12
  ounces (350 g), cut into bite-size
  pieces
4 medium carrots, oblique cut (see
  Hot Tip)
1 block extra-firm tofu, 14 ounces
  (400 g), drained and cut into 1-inch
  (2.5 cm) cubes
Steamed Japanese Rice, for serving

Japanese curry is strong in flavor but has a subtle sweetness and isn't very spicy, so kids tend to like it over traditional curries. The low-and-slow method of cooking the stew meat in this recipe breaks it down, leaving it juicy and tender — so don't bother getting higher-grade cuts of meat, or the reverse will happen and you will end up with tough meat. Add any vegetables to this hot pot, like bean sprouts, Napa cabbage and shiitake mushrooms, but to please my kids, I've included only what they like in this one.

1 Season the beef with salt and pepper and dust with flour.

2 In a 4-quart (3.8 L) hot pot or large saucepan over medium-high heat, (about 425°F, or 220°C, in an electric hot pot), heat the olive oil. Add half the beef and cook, turning occasionally, until browned, about 6 minutes then transfer to a bowl. Cook the remaining beef in the same way with more olive oil, if needed. Return the cooked beef to the pot.

3 Add the Japanese curry broth and bring to a boil. Reduce the heat to low, cover the pot and simmer for 1 hour.

4 Add the potatoes and carrots. Cover the pot and cook for a further 45 minutes.

5 Add the tofu. Cover and cook until the meat and vegetables are tender and the tofu is heated through, about 15 minutes more.

6 Ladle into shallow bowls and serve with steamed rice.

HOT TIP

To make an oblique cut:

1. Peel the carrots and cut off the stems.

2. Hold each carrot on a cutting surface with your non-dominant hand and hold the knife with your dominant hand at a 45-degree angle.

3. Cutting about 1-inch (2.5 cm) slices on the diagonal, roll the carrot a quarter turn toward you after each cut. Repeat until the carrot is completely cut. The cuts should be angled toward each other.

Short Rib Sesame Miso Broth Hot Pot

SKILL LEVEL: Moderate
PREP TIME: 20 minutes
COOK TIME: 20 minutes
YIELD: 4 to 6 servings
PREPARATION: At the table

TO MAKE IN ADVANCE

Sesame Miso Broth (page 32)
Sweet-and-Sour Layu Chili Sauce
  (page 37)
Steamed Japanese Rice (page 38)

INGREDIENTS

1½ pounds (680 g) boneless beef
  short ribs, very thinly sliced (see
  Hot Tips)
8 ounces (220 g) baby red potatoes,
  thinly sliced
6 small stalks Chinese broccoli, or
  broccolini, trimmed
3 ounces (85 g) ronfun (white)
  shimeji mushrooms, or enoki
  mushrooms, cleaned and trimmed
2 cups (140 g) packed very thinly
  sliced white cabbage
2 quarts (1.9 L) Sesame Miso Broth
  (see Hot Tips)
Steamed Japanese Rice, for serving
Sweet-and-Sour Layu Chili Sauce, for
  dipping
Julienned scallions, for garnish

The boneless short ribs in this recipe are incredibly tender and soak up the flavor of the sesame miso broth really well. You could get away with no dipping sauce, but the Sweet-and-Sour Layu Chili Sauce takes it to another level. Look for well-marbled short ribs for beef that will melt in your mouth.

1 Arrange the beef, potatoes, Chinese broccoli, mushrooms and cabbage on platters. Place the platters on the table around the hot pot.

2 Heat a 4-quart (3.8 L) hot pot or large saucepan over medium-high heat (about 425°F, or 220°C, in an electric hot pot). Add the sesame miso broth and bring to a boil.

3 Let everyone add their own meat, vegetables and tofu, swishing back and forth in the hot broth until the vegetables are tender and the meat is still slightly pink, 1 to 2 minutes. As food is added, adjust the heat to maintain a low boil.

4 Serve with the steamed rice on the side and the layu chili sauce for dipping. Garnish with the scallions.

HOT TIPS

► Freeze the beef up to 4 hours so it is firm and easier to slice or purchase sukiyaki or shabu-shabu beef at Asian markets or ask your butcher to thinly slice it.

► This recipe is easy to scale up or down. Just make sure your hot pot is filled about halfway with broth. If the liquid reduces over time, add more.

Pork
Hot Pots

Pork Sukiyaki

SKILL LEVEL: Moderate
PREP TIME: 20 minutes
COOK TIME: 15 minutes
YIELD: 4 to 6 servings
PREPARATION: At the table

TO MAKE IN ADVANCE
Basic Sukiyaki Sauce (page 36)

INGREDIENTS

1 pound (450 g) pork loin, very thinly sliced (see Hot Tip)

6 ounces (170 g) Chinese green beans, or regular green beans, trimmed and cut diagonally into 2-inch (5 cm) pieces

5 ounces (140 g) king trumpet mushrooms, brown cremini mushrooms, or enoki mushrooms cleaned and trimmed, and sliced or torn into pieces

3 baby bok choy, quartered lengthwise

1 small purple daikon radish, or ½ medium white daikon radish, peeled and thinly sliced

1 block extra-firm tofu, 14 ounces (400 g), drained and cut into 1-inch (2.5 cm) cubes

4–6 portions packaged white shirataki noodles, drained

2 tablespoons bacon fat, or sesame oil, divided

1 medium shallot, thinly sliced, divided

½ cup (120 ml) Basic Sukiyaki Sauce, divided

Black sesame seeds, for garnish

Sukiyaki is probably my favorite type of hot pot because you can use the Basic Sukiyaki Sauce with any meat and vegetable combination. You can even make it vegetarian and increase the amounts of tofu and vegetables. Eat the finished sukiyaki with a bowl of rice or add noodles directly to the hot pot to soak up all the umami-rich sauce. I'm a big fan of the combination of pork and veggies in this recipe: the crisp green beans and daikon radish go well with the tender pork.

1 Arrange the pork, vegetables (except the shallot), tofu and noodles on platters. Place the platters on the table around the hot pot.

2 In a 4-quart (3.8 L) hot pot or large saucepan over medium-high heat (about 425°F, or 220°C, in an electric hot pot), heat 1 tablespoon of the bacon fat. Add half the shallot. Cook for 2 minutes, stirring, until translucent.

3 Add half the vegetables, tofu and noodles to the pot. Cook for about 2 minutes, stirring occasionally, until the vegetables begin to soften.

4 Arrange half the sliced pork on top of the vegetables. Drizzle with ¼ cup (60 ml) of the sukiyaki sauce.

5 Reduce the heat to medium. Cook for about 1 minute, until the pork begins to turn white. Flip the pork and cook for 1 minute more.

6 Fold the cooked pork into the vegetables and noodles until evenly coated with the sauce. Cook until the pork and vegetables are just tender, about 1 minute more. If food starts to stick to the bottom of the hot pot, reduce the heat and add a little water to cool it down.

7 Transfer the pork sukiyaki to shallow serving bowls. Garnish with black sesame seeds and serve.

8 Repeat the process with the remaining 1 tablespoon bacon fat and shallot, followed by the remaining vegetables, tofu, noodles, pork and ¼ cup (60 ml) sukiyaki sauce.

HOT TIP
Freeze the pork up to 4 hours so it is firm and easier to slice or purchase sukiyaki or shabu-shabu pork at Asian markets or ask your butcher to thinly slice it.

Pork Belly with Vegetables Hot Pot

SKILL LEVEL: Moderate
PREP TIME: 20 minutes, plus 1 hour soaking time
COOK TIME: 20 minutes
YIELD: 4 to 6 servings
PREPARATION: At the table

TO MAKE IN ADVANCE

Pork Bone Broth (page 28)
Sweet-and-Sour Layu Chili Sauce
(page 37)

INGREDIENTS

Ice water, for soaking
½ head radicchio, cut into 1-inch
(2.5 cm) wedges
1 pound (450 g) pork belly, very
thinly sliced (see Hot Tip)
½ large lotus root, peeled and sliced
¼ inch (5 mm) thick
3 medium carrots, julienned
3 ounces (85 g) buna-shimeji
mushrooms or enoki mushrooms,
cleaned and trimmed
1 cup (130 g) Korean rice ovaletts
4–6 servings frozen, cooked udon
noodles, thawed
2 quarts (1.9 L) Pork Bone Broth
Sweet-and-Sour Layu Chili Sauce, for
dipping

This lusciously creamy hot pot is the most soothing dinner on a cold winter night. Here, I use a silky pork bone broth as the base and serve tender, thinly sliced pork belly alongside it for everyone to swish in the hot soup. Nothing compares to juicy, tender pork belly — it adds so much flavor to the broth. If you're able to make this broth over the weekend and buy presliced pork belly at the Asian market, this soup won't take too much time to make on a weeknight for the family.

Another specialty ingredient that truly makes this hot pot shine is the Korean rice ovaletts. They are small, chewy dumpling-like disks made from rice flour and often used in stir-fries and soups. These little cakes have the ideal texture for soaking up whatever flavorful liquid you put them in, making them perfect for hot pots.

1. In a large bowl filled with ice water, soak the radicchio for 1 hour to get rid of its bitterness. Drain well.

2. Arrange the pork belly, vegetables, ovaletts and noodles on platters. Place the platters on the table around the hot pot.

3. Heat a 4-quart (3.8 L) hot pot or large saucepan over medium-high heat (about 425°F, or 220°C, in an electric pot). Add the pork bone broth and bring to a boil.

4. Let everyone add their own pork belly, vegetables and ovaletts to the hot broth, swishing them back and forth until tender and cooked through, 1 to 2 minutes. As food is added, adjust the heat to maintain a low boil. Serve with the layu chili sauce for dipping and steamed rice on the side.

5. When all the pork and vegetables have been eaten, add the udon noodles to the broth. Cook for 2 to 3 minutes, stirring, until heated through. Serve the noodles as the shime (end-of-meal course).

HOT TIP

Freeze the pork up to 4 hours so it is firm and easier to slice or purchase sukiyaki or shabu-shabu pork at Asian markets or ask your butcher to thinly slice it.

Pork Hot Pot with Sesame and Miso

SKILL LEVEL: Moderate
PREP TIME: 30 minutes
COOK TIME: 30 minutes
YIELD: 4 to 6 servings
PREPARATION: At the table

TO MAKE IN ADVANCE

Basic Dashi Stock (page 26)

INGREDIENTS

8 ounces (220 g) pork loin, very thinly sliced (see Hot Tip)

2 cups (200 g) bean sprouts

4 ounces (120 g) fresh shiitake mushrooms, cleaned and stemmed

3 ounces (85 g) buna-shimeji mushrooms or enoki mushrooms, cleaned and trimmed

1 block firm tofu, 14 ounces (400 g) drained and cut into 1-inch (2.5 cm) cubes

2 large scallions, white and light green parts only, cut into 1½-inch (3.5 cm) pieces

¼ head Napa cabbage, cored and thick white parts cut into bite-size pieces

1 bunch shungiku chrysanthemum leaves, or watercress, stemmed

1 large carrot, thinly sliced on the diagonal

4–6 portions packaged white shirataki noodles, drained

5 teaspoons white sesame seeds

1 tablespoon vegetable oil

8 ounces (220 g) ground pork

½ teaspoon garlic powder

2 quarts (1.9 L) Basic Dashi Stock, or dashi made with an instant mix

4 teaspoons red miso paste

4 teaspoons neri goma Japanese sesame paste, or tahini

2 teaspoons soy sauce

1 teaspoon sugar

My brother-in-law Victor told me that I had to meet his neighbor Kiko Asaoka. He said I would be amazed by her knowledge of Japanese cooking. I learned she had traveled the world extensively as a diplomat's wife and often entertained and cooked for guests. This recipe, along with others in this book that Kiko has shared with me, are an extension of her devotion to preserving the freshness and natural quality of an ingredient without it being over-seasoned. For the toasty, nutty sesame flavor in this pork hot pot, Kiko uses both ground and roasted white sesame seeds and a sesame paste. The paste, called neri goma, uses seeds that are roasted much longer than those used to make tahini, resulting in a richer, more savory flavor that pairs perfectly with pork; however, if you can't find it, use tahini.

1 Arrange the sliced pork, vegetables, noodles and tofu on platters. Place the platters on the table around the hot pot.

2 In a medium skillet over low heat, toast the sesame seeds for about 10 minutes, stirring, until fragrant and golden brown. Transfer to a mortar with a pestle or a clean coffee grinder and crush the toasted seeds into a fine powder. Wipe out the skillet.

3 In a 4-quart (3.8 L) hot pot or large saucepan over medium-high heat (about 425°F, or 220°C, in an electric pot), heat the vegetable oil. Add the ground pork and the garlic powder. Cook for about 10 minutes, breaking up the meat with a spoon, until cooked through.

4 Stir in the dashi, miso, neri goma, soy sauce, sugar and ground toasted sesame seeds. Bring to a boil, stirring occasionally. Reduce the heat to low. Simmer for about 5 minutes, until the miso, sesame paste and sugar dissolve.

5 Let everyone add their own sliced pork, vegetables and tofu, swishing back and forth in the hot broth until tender and cooked through, 1 to 2 minutes. As food is added, adjust the heat to maintain a low boil.

6 After the meat, vegetables and tofu have been eaten, add the shirataki noodles to the broth. Cook for 2 to 3 minutes, stirring, until heated through. Serve the noodles as the shime (end-of-meal course).

Pork Wontons with Macanese Broth

SKILL LEVEL: Moderate
PREP TIME: 20 minutes
COOK TIME: 20 minutes
YIELD: 6 servings
PREPARATION: Stovetop

TO MAKE IN ADVANCE

Macanese Broth (page 35)
Mom's Crispy Pork Wontons (page 126), in their assembled but uncooked state at the end of Step 6 on page 127.

INGREDIENTS

1 tablespoon vegetable oil
½ medium Vidalia onion, thinly sliced
2 black garlic cloves, or regular garlic cloves, chopped (see Hot Tips)
2 quarts (1.9 L) Macanese Broth (see Hot Tips)
24 Mom's Crispy Pork Wontons, uncooked
3 baby bok choy, quartered lengthwise
3 ounces (85 g) enoki mushrooms, cleaned and trimmed
1 sweet potato, peeled and shredded; or 6 ounces (170 g) spiralized sweet potato
2 large scallions, white and light green parts only, cut diagonally into 2-inch (5 cm) lengths
1 block firm tofu, 14 ounces (400 g), drained and cut into 1-inch (2.5 cm) cubes

In Colorado, where I live, the weather is always a topic of conversation. One day it's bright and sunny and you want to wear flip-flops, and the next day you're bundling up with a beanie on and it's snowing. It was one of the last snowy days in late spring when I first made this hot pot for my family. We made the wontons together, and I told them how I used to make them with my family for our church fair when I was growing up. My kids always enjoy eating and trying new things when they participate in the cooking, so they loved this hot pot — the wontons almost fill with the broth like a soup dumpling, and cook fairly quickly because of the small amount of filling in them. The kids gobbled up their wontons pretty fast, so feel free to add more if you've got little wonton lovers too!

1 In a 4-quart (3.8 L) hot pot or large saucepan over medium-high heat (about 425°F, or 220°C, in an electric pot), heat the vegetable oil. Add the onion. Cook for 4 to 5 minutes, stirring, until translucent. Add the garlic. Cook for about 1 minute, until fragrant.

2 Add the Macanese broth and bring the mixture to a boil.

3 Add the wontons. Reduce the heat to low, cover the pot and simmer for 5 minutes.

4 Add the vegetables and tofu. Cover the pot and cook for 5 minutes more, until the wontons are cooked through and the vegetables are tender.

5 Ladle into shallow bowls and serve.

HOT TIPS

► Black garlic is fermented garlic that is sweet and savory, with a deep molasses-like flavor and a soft consistency. You can find it in specialty food shops and online.

► This recipe is easy to scale up or down. Just make sure your hot pot is filled about halfway with broth. If the liquid reduces over time, add more.

Kurobuta Pork Mille-Feuille Hot Pot

SKILL LEVEL: Easy
PREP TIME: 15 minutes
COOK TIME: 45 minutes
YIELD: 6 to 8 servings
PREPARATION: Stovetop

TO MAKE IN ADVANCE

Vegetable Stock (page 27)
Sesame Miso Sauce (page 38)
Steamed Japanese Rice (page 38)

INGREDIENTS

¼ cup (70 g) white miso paste
¼ cup (70 g) tahini
¼ cup (60 ml) sake or white wine
6 cups (1.4 L) Vegetable Stock,
   or store-bought low-sodium
   vegetable broth
1 piece fresh ginger, about 2 inches
   (5 cm) peeled and finely grated
4 teaspoons soy sauce
2 cups (480 ml) water
2 pounds (900 g) pork belly,
   preferably kurobuta, cut into ¼-
   inch (5-mm)-thick slices
1 head Napa cabbage, cleaned,
   trimmed and leaves separated
3 ounces (85 g) enoki mushrooms,
   cleaned and trimmed
2 fresh shiitake mushrooms,
   cleaned, stemmed and sliced
Sesame Miso Sauce, for dipping
Steamed Japanese Rice, for serving

One of the most beautiful dishes whose recipe was given to me by my friend Emily Lai, this mille-feuille hot pot is a savory Japanese take on the classic French dessert made with thin layers of puff pastry. The layering of the cabbage and pork emulates this French dish, whose name translates to "a thousand leaves." It's a visually appealing dish that is very popular in Japan. It is simple but very tasty because the fatty pork — kurobuta, which comes from a Berkshire pig — is highly marbled and tends to have darker and more flavorful meat. If you can't find kurobuta pork, use any other type of heritage-breed pork to give it that juicy tenderness.

1 In a large saucepan over medium-high heat, combine the miso, tahini, sake, vegetable stock, ginger, soy sauce and water. Whisk to combine. Bring the mixture to a boil. Reduce the heat to low and simmer while you assemble the hot pot, about 15 minutes.

2 Sandwich 1 slice of pork between 2 cabbage leaves. Cut crosswise into three 2- to 3-inch (5 to 7.5 cm) sections and set aside on a work surface.

3 In a 4-quart (3.8 L) hot pot or large saucepan, nestle the cabbage and pork on their sides, cut sides up, in the pot — they should fit snugly. Repeat with the remaining cabbage and pork until all the pork is used up. If you have remaining cabbage leaves, tuck them in around the edges of the pot and anywhere there is a gap. Arrange the mushrooms in the center of the hot pot.

4 Heat the hot pot over medium-high heat (about 425°F, or 220°C, in an electric hot pot) until you can hear the pork and cabbage begin to sizzle, 3 to 4 minutes.

5 Pour the warm broth over the cabbage and pork until just covered and bring to a boil. Cover the pot and reduce the heat to low. Simmer for about 20 minutes, until the cabbage is tender and the pork is cooked through.

6 Serve in shallow bowls with some broth poured over the top, along with the sesame miso sauce for dipping and steamed rice on the side.

Seafood Hot Pots

Soft-Shell Crab in Miso Broth

Soft-shell crabs are not traditionally served in hot pots, but I love their subtle brininess and the way the small crab legs puff up and get crispy when fried. Here, I've broiled the soft-shell crabs so they come out crisp without the grease of deep-frying. Just be careful not to let them soak in the soup too long or they lose their crunch. They only need a quick dunk to heat through. Serve with a side of Shio Koji Pickled Vegetables (page 119).

SKILL LEVEL: Moderate
PREP TIME: 15 minutes
COOK TIME: 30 minutes
YIELD: 4 to 6 servings
PREPARATION: Stovetop

TO MAKE IN ADVANCE

Sesame Miso Broth (page 32)
Ponzu Sauce (page 36)
Steamed Japanese Rice (page 38)

INGREDIENTS

Nonstick cooking spray, preferably
   coconut oil, for greasing
½ cup (60 g) katakuriko Japanese
   potato starch, or cornstarch
12 soft-shell crabs, rinsed (see
   Hot Tips)
5 cups (1.2 L) Sesame Miso Broth
   (see Hot Tips)
2 ears fresh corn, shucked and cut
   into 2-inch (5 cm) pieces
5 ounces (140 g) small fresh shiitake
   mushrooms, cleaned and trimmed
1 bunch karashina Japanese mustard
   cabbage, or arugula
1 large negi Japanese green onion, or
   2 scallions, thinly sliced lengthwise
1 block firm tofu, 14 ounces (400 g),
   drained and cut into 1-inch (2.5 cm)
   cubes
Steamed Japanese Rice, for serving
Ponzu Sauce, for dipping

HOT TIPS

► Soft-shell crabs are usually sold cleaned, so a light rinse is all they need.

► This recipe is easy to scale up or down. Just make sure your hot pot is filled about halfway with broth. If the liquid reduces or thickens over time, add more.

1 Preheat the broiler and position a rack in the middle of the oven. Line a rimmed baking sheet with aluminum foil and coat it with cooking spray. Line another baking sheet with paper towels and set aside.

2 Spread the katakuriko in a shallow bowl. Dredge the crabs in the katakuriko until evenly coated; shake off any excess. Transfer the crabs, bottom sides up, to the baking sheet prepared with cooking spray. Make sure they are not touching. Spray the crabs liberally with cooking spray.

3 On the middle rack, broil the crabs for 8 to 10 minutes, or until they are crispy and golden brown. Watch carefully to make sure they don't burn. Remove the crabs from the oven. Flip them, shell sides up and broil for 5 to 6 minutes more, or until golden and cooked through. Transfer the crabs to the paper towel–lined baking sheet to drain. Arrange the crabs on a platter and place the platter on the table next to the hot pot.

4 Heat a 4-quart (3.8 L) hot pot or large saucepan over medium-high heat (about 425°F, or 220°C, in an electric hot pot). Add the sesame miso broth and bring to a boil.

5 Add the corn to the broth. Cook, turning if not submerged in the broth, until almost tender, about 8 minutes.

6 Add the remaining vegetables and tofu. Cook for about 2 minutes, until the vegetables are tender and the tofu is heated through. Arrange the soft-shell crabs on top of the vegetables so they can soak up some of the broth but are not fully submerged.

7 Transfer to shallow bowls and serve with the steamed rice on the side and the ponzu sauce for dipping.

Poached Salmon Hot Pot

SKILL LEVEL: Moderate
PREP TIME: 30 minutes
COOK TIME: 35 minutes
YIELD: 4 to 6 servings
PREPARATION: Stovetop

TO MAKE IN ADVANCE

Basic Dashi Stock (page 26)
Steamed Japanese Rice (page 38)

INGREDIENTS

1½ pounds (680 g) 1-inch (2.5 cm)-thick, skin-on salmon fillets (preferably Atlantic salmon)
Kosher salt, to taste
Freshly ground black pepper, to taste
1 tablespoon vegetable oil
1 tablespoon sesame oil
½ medium sweet onion, thinly sliced
1 large garlic clove, minced
5 cups (1.2 L) Basic Dashi Stock, or dashi made with an instant mix
2 tablespoons white miso paste
2 tablespoons sake
1½ tablespoons soy sauce
1 tablespoon mirin
1 medium carrot, julienned
½ small satsumaimo sweet potato, or regular sweet potato, peeled and very thinly sliced on a mandoline
3 ounces (85 g) wood ear, shiitake or mushrooms of your choice, cleaned and trimmed
1 cup (100 g) bean sprouts
Steamed Japanese Rice, for serving

My friend Elisabeth Saucier is a fantastic recipe-testing partner: she's a great cook with discerning taste buds and she's not afraid to give me honest feedback. While we were working on this recipe together, Elisabeth had the brilliant idea of gently cooking the salmon separately, and then topping each bowl of steaming soup with the still-pink-inside fish, to poach gently in the broth to tender perfection.

I also love adding greens to this hot pot for a burst of color and some extra vitamins — try 5 ounces (140 g) of chopped asparagus and a cup of baby spinach leaves.

1 Season the salmon fillets with salt and pepper. Line a plate with paper towels and set aside.

2 Heat the vegetable oil in a large nonstick skillet over medium-high heat until shimmering. Add the salmon fillets, skin sides down. Cover the skillet and cook for about 5 minutes, until the salmon is opaque on the outside and still a bit raw on the inside. Uncover the skillet and cook for about 1 minute, until the skin gets a little more crispy — this will make it easier to remove the skin. Transfer the salmon to a plate, skin sides up.

3 Using a paring knife, gently remove the skin from the salmon. Return the skin to the skillet and cook over medium-high heat until very crispy on both sides, about 1 minute per side. Transfer the crispy salmon skins to the paper towel–lined plate to drain. Season them with salt. Cut the salmon skins into small strips to use as a topping.

4 In a 4-quart (3.8 L) hot pot or large saucepan over medium-high heat (about 425°F, or 220°C, in an electric hot pot), heat the sesame oil until shimmering. Add the onion. Cook for about 4 minutes, stirring, until lightly browned. Add the garlic. Cook for about 1 minute until fragrant.

5 Add the dashi, miso, sake, soy sauce and mirin, stirring to dissolve the miso. Bring to a boil. Reduce the heat to a simmer. Add the carrot and sweet potato to the pot. Simmer for 5 minutes.

6 Add the mushrooms and bean sprouts. Simmer until the vegetables are tender, about 5 minutes more. Cut the salmon into 1-inch-thick (2.5 cm) pieces.

7 Ladle the soup and vegetables into shallow bowls. Top each bowl with 3 or 4 pieces of salmon and garnish with the crispy salmon skin. The salmon will continue to cook in the hot soup. Serve with the steamed rice on the side.

Crab Legs and Tofu in Pork Bone Broth

SKILL LEVEL: Moderate
PREP TIME: 20 minutes
COOK TIME: 15 minutes
YIELD: 4 to 6 servings
PREPARATION: At the table

TO MAKE IN ADVANCE

Pork Bone Broth, spicy (page 28)
Chirizu Sauce (page 37)
Steamed Japanese Rice (page 38)

INGREDIENTS

1½ pounds (680 g) cooked crab legs,
  separated
5 ounces (140 g) maitake
  mushrooms, or oyster mushrooms,
  cleaned, trimmed and torn into
  large pieces
1½ cups (30g) loosely packed
  stemmed arugula
1½ cups (45 g) loosely packed fresh
  baby spinach
½ large heirloom tomato, cut into
  ¼-inch-thick (5 mm) wedges
1 block firm tofu, 14 ounces (400 g),
  drained and cut into 1-inch (2.5 cm)
  cubes
4–6 portions packaged white
  shirataki noodles, drained
2 quarts (1.9 L) Pork Bone Broth,
  spicy (see Hot Tip)
Finely chopped jalapeño pepper, for
  garnish, optional
Shichimi togarashi spice blend, or
  red pepper flakes, for garnish
Steamed Japanese Rice, for serving
Chirizu Sauce, for dipping

This hot pot is not only delicious but a real visual stunner. The coral-hued crab legs, ombré maitake mushrooms, crisp greens, clean white noodles and tofu, and the spectrum of reds and greens on an heirloom tomato are a teaser for how bright and complex this dish tastes. I chose to use crab legs versus whole crab because they're easier to crack open, and you can pull out a nice big piece of meat with your chopsticks. I like to serve this with a zesty Chirizu Sauce; it gives a nice balance to the sweet crab and the spice of the pork bone broth.

1 Using a chef's knife, cut the crab legs in half crosswise. Then, using kitchen shears, cut a slit along each shell for easier eating. Arrange the crab, vegetables, tofu and noodles on platters. Place the platters on the table around the hot pot. Provide extra dishes for the discarded crab shells.

2 Heat a 4-quart (3.8 L) hot pot or large saucepan over medium-high heat (about 425°F, or 220°C, in an electric pot). Add the spicy pork bone broth and bring to a boil.

3 Let everyone add their own crab, vegetables, tofu and noodles, swishing each ingredient back and forth in the hot broth until tender and cooked through, 1 to 2 minutes. As food is added, adjust the heat to maintain a low boil. Garnish with the jalapeño and shichimi togarashi and serve with the steamed rice on the side and the chirizu sauce for dipping.

HOT TIP

This recipe is easy to scale up or down. Just make sure the hot pot is filled about halfway with broth. If the liquid reduces over time, add more.

Seafood Medley Shabu-Shabu

SKILL LEVEL: Moderate
PREP TIME: 30 minutes
COOK TIME: 15 minutes
YIELD: 4 to 6 servings
PREPARATION: At the table

TO MAKE IN ADVANCE

Basic Shabu-Shabu Broth (page 29)
Steamed Japanese Rice (page 38)
Ponzu Sauce (page 36)

INGREDIENTS

4-6 portions frozen, cooked udon
noodles, thawed
12–16 large shrimp, about 1 pound
(450 g), shell-on, deveined
1 pound (450 g) littleneck clams,
scrubbed
6 large sea scallops, rinsed and
patted dry
8 ounces (220 g) skinless sea bass or
cod, cut into 2-inch (5 cm) pieces
5 ounces (140 g) oyster mushrooms,
cleaned, trimmed and torn into
small bunches
5 ounces (140 g) forest nameko
mushrooms, or enoki mushrooms,
cleaned, trimmed and torn into
small bunches
1 leek, white part only, cleaned,
quartered and cut into 2-inch
(5 cm) lengths
4 Napa cabbage leaves, cut into
bite-size pieces
1 block firm tofu, 14 ounces (400 g),
drained and cut into 1-inch (2.5 cm)
cubes
2 quarts (1.9 L) Basic Shabu-Shabu
Broth (see Hot Tip)
1 piece fresh ginger, about 1½ inches
(3.5 cm), peeled and thinly sliced
1 tablespoon sesame oil
Steamed Rice, for serving
Ponzu Sauce, for serving

It's important to know that all shabu-shabu starts with a fairly bland broth — it's the ingredients that you gently swish in the broth that add the real flavor. For this seafood-based shabu-shabu, buy the highest-quality fish and shellfish you can find. This dish is a celebration of food in its simplest and most natural form, so you want every ingredient to be fresh and at its most flavorful. I have accompanied this delicate hot pot with a classic, bright and citrusy ponzu sauce. When all the seafood and vegetables have been eaten, the remaining broth can be sipped on its own or you can add rice to make a porridge for the shime (end-of-meal course).

1 Arrange the noodles, seafood, vegetables, and tofu on platters. Place the platters on the table around the hot pot.

2 Heat a 4-quart (3.8 L) hot pot or large saucepan over medium-high heat (about 425°F, or 220°C, in an electric hot pot). Add the shabu-shabu broth, ginger and sesame oil and bring to a boil.

3 Let everyone add their own seafood, vegetables, tofu and noodles, swishing back and forth in the hot broth until the noodles and tofu are warm, the vegetables are tender and the seafood is just cooked: about 6 minutes for the clams, 1 minute for the shrimp and scallops and about 2 minutes for the fish. If any clams do not open, discard and do not eat them. As food is added, adjust the heat to maintain a low boil.

4 Serve with the steamed rice and the ponzu sauce for dipping.

HOT TIP

This recipe is easy to scale up or down. Just make sure your hot pot is filled about halfway with broth. If the liquid reduces over time, add more.

Tuna in Clear Dashi Broth

SKILL LEVEL: Moderate
PREP TIME: 20 minutes
COOK TIME: 10 minutes
YIELD: 4 to 6 servings
PREPARATION: At the table

TO MAKE IN ADVANCE

Basic Dashi Stock (page 26)
Chirizu Sauce (page 37)
Steamed Japanese Rice (page 38)

INGREDIENTS

1 pound (450 g) quality tuna belly (such as ahi), sliced ¼ inch (5 mm) thick (see Hot Tips)

5 ounces (140 g) maitake mushrooms, trimmed and torn into large pieces

3 ounces (85 g) mizuna Japanese mustard greens, stemmed (see Hot Tips)

1 large carrot, shaved into thin ribbons with a vegetable peeler

½ purple daikon radish, about 6 ounces (170 g), peeled and very thinly sliced on a mandoline

¼ head Napa cabbage, cored and thick white parts cut into bite-size pieces

4–6 portions packaged white shirataki noodles, drained

2 quarts (1.9 L) Basic Dashi Stock, or dashi made with an instant mix (see Hot Tips)

2 large scallions, white and light green parts, thinly sliced

2 tablespoons yuzu juice, bottled or fresh, or the juice of ½ lemon and ½ lime

1 tablespoon soy sauce

1 teaspoon kosher salt

Steamed Japanese Rice, for serving

Chirizu Sauce, for dipping

This hot pot is a perfect midday meal or light dinner because it won't weigh you down with spice or richness. The tuna only needs a few seconds in the dashi — you want it to be tender and raw inside. I also love the Chirizu Sauce paired with this hot pot; it's bright and acidic, a natural complement to the tuna that doesn't overpower it.

1 Arrange the tuna, vegetables and noodles on platters. Place the platters on the table around the hot pot.

2 Heat a 4-quart (3.8 L) hot pot or large saucepan over medium-high heat (about 425°F, or 220°C, in an electric hot pot). Add the dashi, scallions, yuzu juice, soy sauce and salt. Bring to a boil.

3 Let everyone add their own tuna, vegetables and noodles, swishing back and forth in the hot broth until the tuna is still slightly raw, just 3 to 5 seconds, and the vegetables and noodles are tender and warmed through, 1 to 2 minutes. As food is added, adjust the heat to maintain a low boil.

4 Serve with steamed rice on the side and the chirizu sauce for dipping.

HOT TIPS

► Refrigerate the tuna up to 4 hours ahead of time so it is firm and easier to slice.

► If you cannot find mizuna, use regular mustard greens. Stem the leaves and cut each leaf into quarters for nice, large pieces.

► This recipe is easy to scale up or down. Just make sure your hot pot is filled about halfway with broth. If the liquid reduces over time, add more.

Vegetable Hot Pots

Green Vegetables in Creamy Corn Broth

SKILL LEVEL: Easy
PREP TIME: 20 minutes
COOK TIME: 15 minutes
YIELD: 4 to 6 servings
PREPARATION: At the table

TO MAKE IN ADVANCE

Creamy Corn Broth (page 30)
Sesame Miso Sauce (page 38)
Steamed Japanese Rice (page 38)

INGREDIENTS

5 ounces (140 g) asparagus, trimmed and cut diagonally into 2-inch (5 cm) pieces
6 curly kale leaves, stemmed and halved lengthwise
3 baby bok choy, quartered lengthwise
2 small broccoli crowns, cut into bite-size florets
2 quarts (1.9 L) Creamy Corn Broth (see Hot Tip)
Snipped fresh chives, for garnish
Steamed Japanese Rice, for serving
Sesame Miso Sauce, for dipping

This is the perfect hot pot for those times when you need a good dose of heart-healthy green vegetables, but still want something warm and satisfying. It's light enough to serve at lunchtime and comes together quickly as the vegetable preparation is fairly simple. I've chosen green vegetables, such as broccoli and asparagus, that maintain their crisp, natural state even after a few minutes in the sweet and creamy corn broth.

1 Arrange the vegetables on a platter. Place the platter on the table around the hot pot.

2 Heat a 4-quart (3.8 L) hot pot or large saucepan over medium-high heat (about 425°F, or 220°C, in an electric hot pot). Add the creamy corn broth and bring to a boil.

3 Let everyone add their own vegetables, swishing back and forth for a few minutes in the hot broth until tender and cooked through, 1 to 2 minutes. As food is added, adjust the heat to maintain a low boil.

4 Garnish the cooked vegetables with the chives and serve with the steamed rice on the side and the sesame miso sauce for dipping.

HOT TIP

This recipe is easy to scale up or down. Just make sure your hot pot is filled about halfway with broth. If the liquid reduces over time, add more.

Vegetarian Rice Congee Hot Pot

SKILL LEVEL: Moderate
PREP TIME: 30 minutes
COOK TIME: 40 minutes
YIELD: 6 to 8 servings
PREPARATION: Stovetop

TO MAKE IN ADVANCE

Vegetable Stock (page 27)

INGREDIENTS

FOR THE BROTH

4 garlic cloves, peeled
3 shallots, peeled
2 tablespoons vegetable oil
1 piece fresh ginger, about 4 inches
   (10 cm), peeled and thinly sliced
6 lemongrass stalks, tough outer
   layers removed, crushed and cut
   into 4-inch (10 cm) pieces
10 cups (2.4 L) Vegetable Stock,
   or store-bought low-sodium
   vegetable broth
1½ cups (300 g) uncooked short-
   grain brown rice, rinsed well
1½ cups (300 g) uncooked short-
   grain white rice, rinsed well
Kosher salt, to taste
Ground white pepper, to taste

FOR THE HOT POT

1 block firm tofu, about 14 ounces
   (400 g), drained and cut into 1-inch
   (2.5 cm) pieces
4 rectangular pieces aburaage
   fried tofu
1 bunch yuba dried bean curd sticks,
   hydrated for 10 minutes in boiling
   water
¼ head Napa cabbage, cored and
   thick white parts cut into bite-size
   pieces
5 ounces (140 g) enoki mushrooms,
   cleaned, trimmed and torn into
   small bunches
Soy sauce, for drizzling
Sesame oil, for drizzling
Fried shallots (store-bought is fine),
   for garnish

My friend Emily Lai has two kids and lots of nieces and nephews, so she's used to making adjustments for kids and making sure her meals are super kid-friendly. She told me that congee is an introductory food for many Asian toddlers, so the textures and flavors in this dish are not foreign to them. Your kids will like the mild flavors of the broth — it's like a warm, filling porridge. Don't forget to wash the rice to remove all the impurities before cooking it, and feel free to improvise and add the veggies you prefer!

1 To make the broth: In a food processor, pulse the garlic and shallots until finely chopped.

2 Heat the vegetable oil in a large skillet over medium-high heat. Add the ginger and lemongrass. Cook for about 2 minutes, until fragrant. Add the chopped garlic and shallots. Cook for about 2 minutes more, until softened.

3 Add the vegetable stock and bring to a boil.

4 Add the brown and white rice. Cover the skillet, reduce the heat to low and simmer until thickened, stirring occasionally, about 20 minutes. If the congee gets too thick, add ½ cup (120 ml) water. Remove and discard the lemongrass.

5 Using an immersion blender, or in a standard blender and working in batches, puree the congee until it is smooth and has a porridge-like consistency. Season with salt and pepper.

6 To make the hot pot: Heat a 4-quart (3.8 L) hot pot or large saucepan over medium-high heat (about 425°F, or 220°C, in an electric hot pot). Add the congee and bring to a boil. Reduce the heat to maintain a simmer.

7 Add the tofu, yuba, cabbage and mushrooms to the pot. Continue simmering for 10 minutes.

8 Ladle the congee into shallow bowls and drizzle with the soy sauce and sesame oil. Garnish with the fried shallots.

Mixed Vegetables in Soy Milk Broth

SKILL LEVEL: Moderate
PREP TIME: 20 minutes
COOK TIME: 20 minutes
YIELD: 4 to 6 servings
PREPARATION: Stovetop

TO MAKE IN ADVANCE

Soy Milk Broth (page 29)
Steamed Japanese Rice (page 38)

INGREDIENTS

2 quarts (1.9 L) Soy Milk Broth (see Hot Tip)
1 medium carrot, sliced
3 medium sized Yukon Gold potatoes, peeled and cut into 1 inch (2.5 cm) cubes
1 small broccoli crown, cut into bite-size florets
8 oz (220 g) button mushrooms, washed and sliced
3 small slender Asian eggplants, stemmed and sliced into large chunks
¼ large daikon radish, peeled and thinly sliced, or 6 small radishes, halved
1 large negi Japanese green onion, or 2 scallions, julienned
Steamed Japanese Rice, for serving

The steaming soy milk broth used in this hot pot makes it taste rich and creamy and I like that it's both gluten- and dairy-free. Even though this is a vegetable-only hot pot, the eggplant and the steamed rice make it hearty and filling. Any vegetables can be substituted depending on what's in season — just look for a variety that will give you different textures and colors. This hot pot is perfect for a cold rainy day or a family weekend dinner and it's my idea of comfort in a bowl.

1 Heat a 4-quart (3.8 L) hot pot or large saucepan over medium-high heat (about 425°F, or 220°C, in an electric pot). Add the soy milk broth and bring to a boil.

2 Add the carrot and potatoes to the hotpot. Cover the pot and cook for about 15 minutes, until the carrots and potatoes are almost tender.

3 Add the remaining vegetables. Cook for 5 minutes until everything is cooked through.

4 Transfer to shallow bowls and serve with the steamed rice on the side.

HOT TIP

This recipe is easy to scale up or down. Just make sure your hot pot is filled about halfway with broth. If the liquid reduces over time, add more.

Tofu in Kombu Dashi Hot Pot

SKILL LEVEL: Moderate
PREP TIME: 20 minutes
COOK TIME: 10 minutes
YIELD: 4 servings
PREPARATION: Stovetop

TO MAKE IN ADVANCE

Steamed Japanese Rice (page 38)

INGREDIENTS

1 large piece dried kombu seaweed, about 20 inches (50 cm) square

4 cups (960 ml) room-temperature water

⅔ cup (160 ml) soy sauce

½ teaspoon dried bonito flakes

2 blocks firm silken tofu, each 14 ounces (400 g), drained and cut into 1-inch (2.5 cm) cubes

3 large scallions, white and light green parts only, thinly sliced

Steamed Japanese Rice, for serving

This simple, authentically Japanese dish is another one I learned from my friend Kiko. Take care to use room-temperature water when soaking the kombu. If the water is warm or too hot, the kombu develops a slimy, bitter film. The light, kombu-steeped water is the foundation for this dish. Also, keep an eye on the heat so the hot pot doesn't come to a boil. Silken tofu is very delicate and will fall apart if it's cooked at higher than a simmer. Since this simple dish has few ingredients, use the highest-quality tofu you can find, as it will make a big difference in texture and flavor.

1 In a 4-quart (3.8 L) hot pot or large saucepan, cover the kombu with the water. Let soak for 20 minutes. Remove and discard the kombu.

2 In an 8-ounce (240 ml) ramekin, stir together the soy sauce and bonito flakes. Set the ramekin in the center of the hot pot or saucepan, taking care not to let the kombu water spill into the ramekin. If needed, remove some of the kombu water.

3 Arrange the tofu in the pot around the ramekin. Cook over medium heat (425°F, or 220°C, in an electric hot pot) until the tofu and the sauce are heated through, about 8 minutes.

4 Ladle a spoonful of the sauce into 4 shallow bowls and top each with a piece of tofu.

5 Garnish with the scallions and serve with the steamed rice on the side.

Mixed Mushroom and Vegetable Hot Pot

SKILL LEVEL: Moderate
PREP TIME: 20 minutes
COOK TIME: 20 minutes
YIELD: 4 to 6 servings
PREPARATION: At the table

TO MAKE IN ADVANCE

Thai Coconut Curry Broth (page 31)
Steamed Japanese Rice (page 38)

INGREDIENTS

1 pound (450 g) mixed mushrooms, such as fresh shiitake, buna-shimeji, enoki, oyster, wood ear or maitake, cleaned, trimmed and torn into large pieces
½ medium-sized lotus root, peeled and sliced
1 large carrot, shaved into thin ribbons with a vegetable peeler
1 green onion, sliced into 1 inch (2.5 cm) pieces
3 large bok choy, sliced lengthwise
¼ head Napa cabbage, cored and thick white parts cut into bite-size pieces
1 block grilled tofu, about 10 oz (300 g) , drained, cut in half lengthwise and sliced into ¼ inch (5 mm) strips
2 quarts (1.9 L) Thai Coconut Curry Broth (see Hot Tip)
Steamed Japanese Rice, for serving

HOT TIP

This recipe is easy to scale up or down. Just make sure your hot pot is filled about halfway with broth. If the liquid reduces over time, add more.

This creamy, coconut milk–based hot pot is a great way to experiment with all those types of mushrooms available at your farmers' market or grocery store. It's becoming easier to find Japanese mushrooms beyond shiitake, so don't limit yourself. Swap in whatever edible varieties you find — just pick ones that vary in look and size for a more visually interesting dish. After cooking, don't toss out that leftover broth; the coconut curry is so flavorful on its own, you'll want to spoon some over your rice or sip it straight from the bowl.

1 Arrange the vegetables and tofu on platters. Place the platters on the table around the hot pot.

2 Heat a 4-quart (3.8 L) hot pot or large saucepan over medium-high heat (about 425°F, or 220°C, in an electric pot). Add the Thai coconut curry broth and bring to a boil.

3 Let everyone add their own vegetables, swishing back and forth in the hot broth until tender and cooked through, 1 to 2 minutes. As food is added, adjust the heat to maintain a low boil.

4 Serve with the steamed rice.

Spicy Hot Pots

Seafood Tom Yum Hot Pot

This fragrant, Thai-inspired recipe from my chef friend Emily Lai incorporates tom yum paste. On its own, the broth has a hot and sour taste, similar to tom yum soup, but the seafood added to the hot pot gives it a sweet brininess with layers of flavor. In this recipe, Emily gives some ideas for the types of seafood and vegetables to use, but consider it a guideline; use what looks freshest or what you have on hand. My suggestions: instead of black cod, you could use monkfish or bass; instead of shiitake, use shimeji, enoki, or maitake mushrooms.

SKILL LEVEL: Moderate
PREP TIME: 30 minutes
COOK TIME: 25 minutes
YIELD: 6 to 8 servings
PREPARATION: At the table

TO MAKE IN ADVANCE

Tomato Broth (page 32)

INGREDIENTS

FOR THE BROTH
2 tablespoons vegetable oil
1 piece fresh ginger, about 4 inches (10 cm), peeled, sliced and smashed
1 piece fresh galangal, about 3 inches (7.5 cm), thinly sliced
6 lemongrass stalks, tough outer layers removed, crushed and cut into 4-inch (10 cm) pieces
4 garlic cloves, minced
3 shallots, minced
2 quarts (1.9 L) water
¼ cup (70 g) tom yum paste (see Hot Tip)
10 kaffir lime leaves, crushed
4 tomatoes, cut into eighths
2 tablespoons fish sauce

3 bird's-eye chilis, optional
2 tablespoons fresh lime juice (from 1 lime)

FOR THE HOT POT
9 ounces (255 g) dried rice noodles
Boiling water, to soak the noodles
1 pound (450 g) crab, cooked or raw, cut into pieces
8 ounces (220 g) littleneck clams, scrubbed
8 ounces (220 g) mussels, scrubbed and debearded (discard any cracked or open mussels)
6–8 large shrimp, about 8 ounces (220 g), shelled, tails on and deveined
4 ounces (120 g) calamari legs
8 ounces (220 g) black cod, skin removed and cut into large pieces
3 baby bok choy, quartered lengthwise
4 Napa cabbage leaves, cut into bite-size pieces
4 ounces (120 g) fresh shiitake mushrooms, cleaned and trimmed
Fresh Thai basil leaves, for garnish
Fresh cilantro leaves, for garnish

1. To make the broth: In a 4-quart (3.8 L) hot pot or large saucepan over medium-high heat (about 425°F, or 220°C, in an electric hot pot), heat the vegetable oil. Add the ginger, galangal and lemongrass. Cook for about 2 minutes, stirring, until fragrant. Add the garlic and shallots. Cook until softened, about 2 minutes more.

2. Add the water, tom yum paste, lime leaves, tomatoes, fish sauce and chilis (if using). Bring to a boil. Reduce the heat to a simmer and cook for 20 minutes. When ready to eat, increase the heat to medium-high and return the broth to a boil. Stir in the lime juice.

3. To make the hot pot: Place the dried rice noodles in a large heat-proof bowl. Cover with the boiling water and let sit for about 10 minutes, until tender and pliable. Rinse under cold water and drain well.

4. Arrange the seafood, fish, vegetables and noodles on platters. Place the platters on the table around the hot pot.

5. Let everyone add their own seafood, fish, vegetables and noodles, swishing back and forth in the hot broth until the noodles are warmed through, the vegetables are tender and the seafood is just cooked through: about 6 minutes for the crab, clams and mussels; about 2 minutes for the fish, and about 1 minute for the shrimp and calamari. If any clams or mussels do not open, discard and do not eat them. As food is added, adjust the heat to maintain a low boil.

6. Ladle the soup into shallow bowls, garnish with the basil and cilantro and serve.

HOT TIP

Tom yum paste is typically made from lemongrass, shallots, garlic, kaffir lime leaves, galangal, lime juice, fish sauce, red pepper flakes and soybean oil. There are multiple varieties, so look for one rich in color and made in Thailand. You can find it at Asian markets and online.

Mongolian Lamb Hot Pot

SKILL LEVEL: Moderate
PREP TIME: 20 minutes
COOK TIME: 15 minutes
YIELD: 4 to 6 servings
PREPARATION: At the table

TO MAKE IN ADVANCE

Mongolian Broth (page 33)
Sesame Miso Sauce (page 38)
Steamed Japanese Rice (page 38)

INGREDIENTS

1 pound (450 g) boneless lamb, very thinly sliced (see Hot Tips)

3 baby bok choy, quartered lengthwise

4 ounces (120 g) Chinese broccoli, washed and stemmed

3 ounces (85 g) enoki mushrooms, cleaned and trimmed

1 large tomato, cut into ½-inch-thick (1 cm) wedges and seeded

½ watermelon radish, peeled and thinly sliced on a mandoline

¼ small kabocha pumpkin, with peel on, seeded and thinly sliced

4 rectangular pieces aburaage fried tofu, sliced ¼ inch (5 mm) thick

1 block firm tofu, 14 ounces (400 g), drained and cut into 1-inch (2.5 cm) pieces

4–6 servings uncooked, fresh ramen noodles

2 quarts (1.9 L) Original or Spicy Mongolian Broth; or 4 cups (960 ml) Original Mongolian Broth and 4 cups (960 ml) Spicy Mongolian Broth

Steamed Japanese Rice, for serving

Sesame Miso Sauce, for dipping

Most Mongolian hot pot restaurants usually offer three options: original, spicy, or half-and-half. I always prefer a traditional split pot because it gives those eating the freedom to choose. The aromatics in the broths complement the lamb and mellow any gaminess, while the sesame miso sauce is the perfect savory finish for both meat and vegetables.

1 Arrange the lamb, vegetables, tofu and noodles on platters. Place the platters on the table around the hot pot.

2 Heat a 4-quart (3.8 L) hot pot or large saucepan over medium-high heat (about 425°F, or 220°C, in an electric hot pot). Add the Mongolian broth. If you are using a split hot pot and serving both original and spicy broths, repeat on the other side with the spicy Mongolian broth. Bring to a boil.

3 Let everyone add their own lamb, vegetables, tofu and noodles, swishing back and forth for a few minutes in the hot broth until each item is tender and cooked through. As food is added, adjust the heat to maintain a low boil.

4 Serve with the steamed rice on the side and the sesame miso sauce for dipping.

HOT TIPS

► Freeze the lamb up to 4 hours until it is firm and easier to slice or purchase sukiyaki or shabu-shabu lamb at Asian markets or ask your butcher to thinly slice it.

► This recipe is easy to scale up or down. Just make sure your hot pot is filled about halfway with broth. If the liquid reduces over time, add more.

Mussels in Spicy Tomato Broth

SKILL LEVEL: Moderate
PREP TIME: 20 minutes
COOK TIME: 10 minutes
YIELD: 4 to 6 servings
PREPARATION: At the table

TO MAKE IN ADVANCE

Tomato Broth (page 32, spicy version, following instructions in step 3)

INGREDIENTS

2 quarts (1.9 L) Tomato Broth, spicy (see Hot Tip)

2 pounds (900 g) mussels, scrubbed and debearded (discard any cracked or open mussels)

4 rectangular pieces aburaage fried tofu, sliced ¼ inch (5 mm) thick

3 oz (85 g) shishito peppers, stemmed

1 leek, white part only, cleaned, cut into ¼-inch (5 mm) slices and separated

1 yellow squash, stemmed and cut into ¼-inch (5 mm) slices

1 medium red bell pepper, seeded and sliced

Juice and zest of 1 lemon

2½ ounces (75 g) daikon radish sprouts, or bean sprouts

⅓ cup (3 g) finely chopped fennel or anise fronds, for garnish, optional

Shichimi togarashi spice blend, or red pepper flakes, for sprinkling

This is a comfort hot pot, perfect for a cold day. I like how the spiciness of this dish comes in all different forms — from the red pepper flakes in the tomato broth to the radish sprouts and shishito peppers. The lemon juice and zest add a fresh but subtle zing that perfectly complements the mussels. The mussels leak a briny liquid gold that seeps into the broth and gives it that salty taste of the sea — similar to a bouillabaisse. I was tempted to break off a crusty French loaf and dip it in the remaining soup, but this dish is hearty enough to eat like a stew and surprisingly filling without any carbs. Fennel isn't for everyone, as it has a very distinct flavor (like licorice), but I think it gives this dish a nice balance with fresh, fragrant herbal notes in every bite. This hot pot comes together very quickly, so don't overestimate how much time the mussels need to cook — the veggies and mussels require only 5 minutes!

1 Heat a 4-quart (3.8 L) hot pot or large saucepan over medium-high heat (about 425°F, or 220°C, in an electric pot). Add the spicy tomato broth and bring to a boil.

2 Place the mussels into the broth in the middle of the pot. Surround them with the tofu, followed by the shishito peppers, leek, squash and red bell pepper. Squeeze the lemon juice over everything and sprinkle with the zest. Cover the pot, reduce the heat to low and simmer for 5 minutes, until the mussels open. If any mussels do not open, discard and do not eat them.

3 Right before serving, add the radish sprouts. Serve in shallow bowls. Garnish with the fennel (if using) and sprinkle with the shichimi togarashi for extra spice. Leave everyone an extra bowl for the mussel shells.

HOT TIP

This recipe is easy to scale up or down. Just make sure your hot pot is filled about halfway with broth. If the liquid reduces over time, add more.

Thai Coconut Curry Chicken Hot Pot

SKILL LEVEL: Moderate
PREP TIME: 20 minutes
COOK TIME: 30 minutes
YIELD: 6 to 8 servings
PREPARATION: Stovetop

TO MAKE IN ADVANCE

Thai Coconut Curry Broth (page 31)
Steamed Japanese Rice (page 38)

INGREDIENTS

3 pounds (1.3 kg) boneless, skinless chicken thighs, cut into bite-size pieces
Kosher salt, to taste
Freshly ground black pepper, to taste
2 tablespoons vegetable oil, divided
2 quarts (1.9 L) Thai Coconut Curry Broth (see Hot Tip)
6 baby eggplants (such as Thai or fairy tale), stemmed and quartered, or 1 medium eggplant cut into bite-size pieces)
½ small kabocha pumpkin, seeded and thinly sliced
¼ head Napa cabbage, cored and thick white parts cut into bite-size pieces
1 cup (150 g) cherry tomatoes
2 cups (40 g) loosely packed fresh Thai or regular basil leaves
2–3 stemmed, seeded and minced bird's-eye chilis or Fresno chilis, optional
Steamed Japanese Rice, for serving

The most difficult thing about this recipe was coming up with a name for it. My Thai friend, Katie, explained to me that you cannot call a curry a hot pot in Thailand because they are two separate things. Thai curries are traditionally thicker in consistency, while Thai hot pots are more similar to traditional dashi-based Japanese recipes. I think the creaminess of the coconut milk and the robust profile of curry lend themselves well to hot pots — the meat and vegetables soak up so much of that flavor in a brief time. Here, I use a base that has all the complexity of a creamy Thai curry, but it is thinned out with a bit of chicken broth for swishing your vegetables in.

1 Season the chicken with the salt and pepper.

2 In a large skillet over medium-high heat, heat 1 tablespoon of the vegetable oil. Add half of the chicken. Cook for 4 to 5 minutes, stirring once or twice, until browned, but not cooked through. Transfer to a clean bowl and repeat with the remaining 1 tablespoon oil and chicken.

3 Heat a 4-quart (3.8 L) hot pot or large saucepan over medium-high heat (about 425°F, or 220°C, in an electric hot pot). Add the broth and chicken and bring to a boil. Reduce the heat to medium-low and simmer for 5 minutes.

4 Add the eggplant, kabocha, cabbage and tomatoes. Continue simmering for about 5 minutes more, until the vegetables are tender and the chicken is cooked through. Stir in the basil and chili (if using).

5 Ladle into shallow bowls and serve with the steamed rice on the side.

HOT TIP
This recipe is easy to scale up or down. Just make sure your hot pot is filled about halfway with broth. If the liquid reduces over time, add more.

Vietnamese Oxtail Hot Pot

SKILL LEVEL: Moderate
PREP TIME: 40 minutes
COOK TIME: 2 hours 30 minutes to 3 hours
YIELD: 6 servings
PREPARATION: Stovetop

TO MAKE IN ADVANCE

Vietnamese Broth (page 34)
Sweet-and-Sour Layu Chili Sauce (page 37)

INGREDIENTS

1 cup (120 g) all-purpose flour
6 large oxtails, about 4 pounds (1.8 kg); about 2 inches (5 cm) thick (see Hot Tips)
Kosher salt, to taste
Freshly ground black pepper, to taste
2 tablespoons vegetable oil, plus more as needed
2 quarts (1.9 L) Vietnamese Broth (see Hot Tips)
1 pound (450 g) dried rice noodles
Boiling water, to soak the noodles
Bean sprouts, for garnish
Fresh Thai basil leaves, for garnish
Fresh cilantro leaves and tender stems, for garnish
Thinly sliced jalapeños, for garnish
Lime wedges, for serving
Sweet-and-Sour Layu Chili Sauce, for dipping

This Vietnamese-style hot pot is one of my favorites. It might seem time-consuming, but this recipe is relatively hands-off while you let the oxtails simmer in the aromatic broth until they're incredibly tender. The slow cooking releases the fat from the bone marrow, giving the hot and sour, tom yum–style broth a silky, unctuous mouthfeel. It's a perfect combination of savory and spicy, with a bright, peppery kick from fresh herbs and garnishes inspired by traditional Vietnamese pho noodle soup. The Sweet-and-Sour Layu Chili Sauce is also a nod to the classic pho accompaniments hoisin and sriracha. I like to drizzle a bit of the sauce into my soup to break up the richness, but it's also nice to give everyone a little bowl on the side as a dip for the oxtail meat.

1 Spread the flour in a shallow bowl. Season the oxtails with salt and pepper and dredge them in the flour, shaking off any excess.

2 In a 4-quart (3.8 L) hot pot or large saucepan over medium-high heat (about 425°F, or 220°C, in an electric pot), heat the vegetable oil. Add half the oxtails and cook, turning, until browned all over, 5 to 7 minutes. Transfer to a plate and repeat with the remaining oxtails, adding more oil, if needed.

3 Return the oxtails to the pot. Add the Vietnamese broth, increase the heat to high and bring to a boil. Cover the pot, reduce the heat to low and simmer for 2½ to 3 hours, until the oxtails are tender.

4 Meanwhile, place the dried noodles in a large bowl. Cover the noodles with the boiling water and let sit for 8 to 10 minutes, until tender. Rinse under cold water and drain well.

5 Arrange the bean sprouts, herbs, jalapeños and rice noodles on platters. Place the platters on the table around the hot pot.

6 Ladle the soup into bowls, giving each person an oxtail.

7 Let everyone add their own bean sprouts, herbs, jalapeño and noodles. Serve with the lime wedges and the layu chili sauce for dipping.

HOT TIPS

► Look for high-quality oxtails that have a generous amount of meat surrounding the bone and are on the larger side, so each person will be satisfied with just one.

► This recipe is easy to scale up or down. Just make sure your hot pot is filled about halfway with broth. If the liquid reduces over time, add more.

Korean Short Ribs in Kimchi Broth

SKILL LEVEL: Moderate
PREP TIME: 40 minutes
COOK TIME: 1 hour 10 minutes, plus
30 minutes marinating time
YIELD: 4 to 6 servings
PREPARATION: Stovetop

TO MAKE IN ADVANCE

Kimchi Broth (page 35)

INGREDIENTS

¼ cup (50 g) sugar

2 pounds (900 g) ½-inch (1 cm)-thick
  Korean short ribs

1 cup (240 ml) soy sauce

¼ cup (60 ml) water

2 quarts (1.9 L) Kimchi Broth (see Hot
  Tip)

3 ounces (85 g) ronfun (white)
  shimeji mushrooms, cleaned
  and trimmed

1 block firm tofu, 14 ounces (400 g),
  drained and cut into 1-inch (2.5 cm)
  pieces

1 cup (100 g) bean sprouts

4–6 servings frozen, cooked udon
  noodles, thawed

I'll admit, I'm not a huge fan of kimchi on its own because of its strong smell, heavy garlic flavor and tang — but in this hot pot, the flavors of the kimchi are mellowed by the beef and slow-cooked vegetables, giving a milder yet flavor-packed broth. Also, although it's optional, the crispy Korean Scallion Pancakes (page 128) are the perfect side and add that needed crunch between bites of tender short ribs and stewed vegetables. If you'd like to make this vegetarian, skip the short ribs and add more vegetables and tofu.

1 Rub the sugar on the short ribs to coat them thoroughly on both sides.

2 In a medium bowl, stir together the soy sauce and water. Coat the short ribs in the mixture and refrigerate for 30 minutes to marinate.

3 Heat a 4-quart (3.8 L) hot pot or large saucepan over medium-high heat (about 425°F, or 220°C, in an electric hot pot). Add the kimchi broth and bring to a boil.

4 Arrange the short ribs around the edge of the hot pot. Cover the pot, reduce the heat to low and simmer for about 1 hour, until the ribs are fork-tender. Remove the ribs and cut them into thirds so they are easier to plate. Place them back into the hot pot.

5 Add the mushrooms, tofu and bean sprouts. Cover the pot and simmer for about 5 minutes, until tender.

6 When all the meat and vegetables have been eaten and you are left with just broth, add the noodles. Cook for 2 to 3 minutes, or until heated through. Serve the noodles as the shime (end-of-meal course).

HOT TIP

This recipe is easy to scale up or down. Just make sure your hot pot is filled about halfway with broth. If the liquid reduces over time, add more.

Salads, Snacks & Side Dishes

Simple Salad with Sesame Soy Dressing

SKILL LEVEL: Easy
PREP TIME: 10 minutes
YIELD: 4 servings

INGREDIENTS

¼ cup (60 ml) rice vinegar

¼ cup (70 g) white miso paste

2 tablespoons toasted white sesame
seeds, plus more for garnish

3 tablespoons packed light brown
sugar

¼ cup (60 ml) sesame oil

Kosher salt, to taste

½ large head iceberg lettuce, cored
and thinly sliced

1 medium carrot, shredded

½ ripe Asian pear, peeled, cored and
julienned

1 avocado, halved, pitted, peeled
and thinly sliced

My kids are like most: they don't like "salads made with weeds," which translates to, "We will only eat iceberg or romaine lettuce." So, I created this simple salad that they really enjoy. My son, Ryan, still eats it plain without any dressing, but most kids will enjoy the sweetness of the Asian pear and the savory creaminess of the miso. This dressing is also fantastic on a salad of simple green leaves, as a dip for crudités, or drizzled over half an avocado for a quick snack. You'll have enough dressing for multiple uses, so store it in a jar and keep it on hand in the refrigerator. It will keep for a few weeks.

1 In a small bowl, whisk together the vinegar, miso, sesame seeds and brown sugar until smooth. While whisking constantly, slowly stream in the sesame oil until incorporated. Season with salt.

2 Arrange the lettuce, carrot, pear and avocado on salad plates and drizzle with some of the dressing. Garnish with more sesame seeds.

Shio Koji Pickled Vegetables

SKILL LEVEL: Easy
PREP TIME: 10 minutes, plus 2 hours marinating time
YIELD: 4 to 6 servings

INGREDIENTS

6 tablespoons shio koji
¼ cup (60 ml) fresh lemon juice
2 teaspoons freshly grated
   lemon zest
1 tablespoon sugar
1 teaspoon peppercorns
10 whole cloves
2 dried bay leaves
½ teaspoon red pepper flakes
2 large carrots, peeled and thinly
   sliced on the diagonal
2 large watermelon radishes, thinly
   sliced on a mandoline
1 cup (100 g) peeled and thinly sliced
   (on a mandoline) daikon radish
1 cup (130 g) peeled and thinly sliced
   (on a mandoline) jicama
½ English cucumber, peeled, seeded
   and thinly sliced
8 fresh shiso leaves, halved down
   the middle

One day at a Japanese market here in Boulder, I met a woman named Miko, who offered to make me some of her homemade shio koji, an umami-rich condiment made from salt (shio) and rice that is fermented with koji, the edible fungus used to make miso and sake. Shio koji is perfect with raw vegetables, because it helps bring out their natural sweetness. These quick pickles are best eaten within a couple of hours when the shio koji flavor is stronger and the vegetables haven't released too much liquid. And though you may not know someone like Miko, you can easily find shio koji at Japanese markets and online.

1 In a medium bowl, stir together the shio koji, lemon juice and zest, sugar, peppercorns, cloves, bay leaves and red pepper flakes.

2 Add the vegetables and shiso, and toss to coat.

3 Refrigerate to marinate for at least 2 hours or up to overnight before serving.

Broiled Mochi in Dashi Stock

SKILL LEVEL: Moderate
PREP TIME: 20 minutes
COOK TIME: 10 minutes
YIELD: 6 servings

TO MAKE IN ADVANCE

Basic Dashi Stock (page 26)

INGREDIENTS

Nonstick cooking spray, for preparing the baking sheet

6 kiri mochi blocks, or freshly made maru mochi patties, halved (see Hot Tips)

2 cups Basic Dashi Stock, or dashi made with an instant mix

¼ cup (60 ml) soy sauce

1 piece (2 inches, or 5 cm) fresh ginger, peeled and finely grated

1 tablespoon finely grated peeled daikon radish

Shredded nori seaweed, for garnish

1 large scallion, white and light green parts only, thinly sliced

Carrot flowers, for garnish, optional (see Hot Tips)

Since I was a kid, it has been our New Year's Eve tradition to make freshly pounded mochi rice cakes and then eat them hot, puffed and golden on New Year's Day. The best, and easiest, way to do this is to pop them under the broiler: the mochi becomes light and crispy on the outside and gooey on the inside. This is still an integral part of my family's New Year's routine. These days, I doctor it up with a simple dashi broth with grated ginger, daikon and scallion and serve the crispy mochi floating in the soup like matzo balls. You can make the soup more substantial by adding grilled chicken or kamaboko fish cake.

1 Preheat the broiler and place a rack 5 inches (13 cm) from the heat. Line a rimmed baking sheet with aluminum foil and coat with nonstick cooking spray.

2 Place the mochi on the baking sheet at 2 inch (5 cm) intervals. Broil until the mochi doubles in size and is puffy and golden brown, about 5 minutes. You do not need to turn the mochi.

3 In a small saucepan over high heat, combine the dashi, soy sauce, ginger and daikon and bring to a boil. Reduce the heat to low and simmer, uncovered, for 2 minutes.

4 Divide the dashi broth between 6 small bowls. Top each bowl with 2 pieces of broiled mochi and garnish with nori, scallion and carrot flowers (if using).

HOT TIPS

► Mochi can be found fresh and packaged at most Asian markets, typically in the freezer section. Unlike dessert mochi, this mochi is not flavored, colored, or filled with anything.

► To make carrot flowers, peel one large carrot and slice it ⅛ inch (3 mm) thick. Using a paring knife, cut small notches around the edge of each slice to make it look like a flower.

Shishito Tempura

SKILL LEVEL: Easy
PREP TIME: 10 minutes
COOK TIME: 20 minutes
YIELD: 4 to 6 servings

INGREDIENTS

Vegetable oil, for frying
1 tablespoon shichimi togarashi
   spice blend
1 tablespoon kosher salt
1 cup (120 g) all-purpose flour
1 cup (240 ml) water
3 ice cubes
8 ounces (220 g) shishito peppers

Crunchy tempura goes well with the soft, stewed meats and vegetables of hot pots. I add ice cubes to the tempura batter, so that when added to hot oil, it puffs into a light, crisp coating without burning. I use shishito peppers here because they are bite-size and mild — even kids like them. But be careful — they say one in ten shishito peppers is extra spicy. I say make a game of it: first one to get the spicy pepper does the dishes!

1 Line a plate with paper towels and set aside. Fill a large saucepan or deep-fryer with 1½ inches (3.5 cm) of vegetable oil and heat over medium-high heat to 360°F (180°C). In a small bowl, mix the shichimi togarashi and salt. Set aside.

2 In a medium bowl, whisk together the flour and water until smooth. Add the ice cubes to the batter, whisking as the ice cubes melt.

3 Test the oil by adding a very small amount of batter — it should fry up quickly when hot enough.

4 When the oil is hot, add a small handful of shishito peppers to the batter and toss to coat. One by one, add the battered peppers to the oil. Fry for about 5 minutes, until lightly browned. Using a slotted spoon, transfer the fried peppers to the prepared plate to drain, and sprinkle with the shichimi-togarashi–salt mixture. Repeat with the remaining shishito peppers. Serve immediately.

Spinach Salad with Sesame Sauce

SKILL LEVEL: Easy
PREP TIME: 10 minutes
COOK TIME: 10 minutes
YIELD: 4 servings

INGREDIENTS

2 tablespoons white sesame seeds,
  plus more for garnish
1 tablespoon soy sauce
1 teaspoon sugar
3 tablespoons sesame oil, divided
1 pound (450 g) fresh spinach
  (not baby spinach), cleaned and
  trimmed

HOT TIP

If you use a coffee grinder, don't overprocess the seeds or you'll end up with sesame paste. Stop grinding before the seeds start to release oil or the powder will clump.

This sweet-and-salty sesame-based sauce, served mixed with a vegetable, is called goma-ae in Japanese. It goes well with most vegetables, but this simple spinach version is the one I make the most. For best results, I encourage you to grind your own sesame seeds, but you can also find tubes of ground sesame paste at most Asian markets, or substitute tahini.

1 In a small dry skillet over low heat, toast the sesame seeds for 10 minutes, constantly stirring, until fragrant and golden brown. Let cool, then crush in a mortar with a pestle or in a clean coffee grinder (see Hot Tip).

2 In a medium bowl, mix the crushed sesame seeds, soy sauce and sugar to make the dressing. It should look like a thick paste.

3 Heat 1 tablespoon of the sesame oil in a large skillet over medium-high heat. Add one-third of the spinach and cook for about 3 minutes, stirring, until just wilted. Transfer to a colander set over a bowl. Repeat twice more with the remaining sesame oil and spinach. Let the spinach cool.

4 Once cool enough to handle, use your hands to squeeze out any liquid from the spinach. Add the spinach to the bowl with the dressing and toss to coat. Refrigerate until cooled.

5 Using your hands, squeeze the spinach into 4 tight balls and arrange on 4 small plates. Garnish with sesame seeds and serve.

6 The sesame dressing can be made ahead and stored in the refrigerator for up to 3 days.

Japanese Mushroom Toast

SKILL LEVEL: Easy
PREP TIME: 10 minutes
COOK TIME: 15 minutes
YIELD: 4 to 6 servings

INGREDIENTS

1 tablespoon unsalted butter

3 tablespoons olive oil, divided

1 medium shallot, finely chopped

12 ounces (350 g) mixed Japanese
   mushrooms, cleaned, trimmed and
   chopped

1 tablespoon sesame oil

Kosher salt, to taste

1 small French bread or rustic loaf,
   sliced diagonally ½ inch (1 cm)
   thick

1 tablespoon white miso paste

1 teaspoon soy sauce

¼ teaspoon shichimi togarashi spice
   blend, or red pepper flakes

1 large scallion, white and light
   green parts only, thinly sliced

When we lived in London, I enjoyed all the lovely breakfast places serving toast heaped with vegetables or meat, but my favorite was always a toast overflowing with rich, sautéed wild mushrooms. This recipe is in memory of our time there — with a Japanese twist! I use shiitake, king trumpets, oyster and forest nameko mushrooms, and hit them with savory-sweet miso and spicy shichimi togarashi spice blend. This crunchy toast works as breakfast topped with an over-easy egg, as a light lunch, or with cocktails, halved on the diagonal.

1 Preheat the broiler and arrange a rack 6 inches (15 cm) from the heat. Line a plate with paper towels and set aside.

2 In a medium skillet over medium-high heat, melt the butter with 1 tablespoon of the olive oil. Add the shallot. Cook for 1 minute, stirring, until softened. Add the mushrooms. Cook, stirring occasionally, until tender and browned, about 8 minutes. Stir in the sesame oil. Season lightly with salt and transfer to the prepared plate to drain.

3 Brush the bread with the remaining 2 tablespoons olive oil. Place the slices on a rimmed baking sheet and broil, turning once, until golden brown.

4 In a small bowl, whisk together the miso, soy sauce and shichimi togarashi. Fold in the mushrooms.

5 Spoon the mushrooms onto the toasts and garnish with the scallion.

Chicken Karaage Nuggets

SKILL LEVEL: Moderate
PREP TIME: 15 minutes, plus 2 to 8 hours marinating time
COOK TIME: 30 minutes
YIELD: 6 to 8 servings

INGREDIENTS

6 tablespoons soy sauce
2 tablespoons agave nectar
2 tablespoons sake
1 piece fresh ginger, about 1½ inches (3.5 cm), peeled and finely grated
2 large garlic cloves, minced
2 large scallions, white parts only, thinly sliced; green parts reserved for garnish
½ teaspoon kosher salt
¼ teaspoon freshly ground black pepper
8 boneless, skinless chicken thighs, about 2½ pounds (1.1 kg) total, each cut into 4 or 5 uniform pieces
Vegetable oil, for frying
3½ cups (210 g) panko bread crumbs
2 large eggs
Lemon wedges, for garnish

This recipe — known as "Chicken Delicious" in our house — started as my attempt at making chicken karaage, Japanese-style fried chicken. The chicken is dredged in katakuriko (Japanese potato starch) and deep-fried, twice. The result is fried chicken that stays shatteringly crunchy for hours. Because I believe frying chicken once is enough, and after much trial and error, the key ingredient turned out to be panko bread crumbs. My kids loved this, gobbled it right up, and said, "Mom, this chicken is delicious!"

1 In a medium bowl, whisk together the soy sauce, agave, sake, ginger, garlic, scallions, salt and pepper until smooth. Add the chicken to the marinade. Refrigerate to marinate for at least 2 hours or overnight.

2 Line a rimmed baking sheet with foil and place a cooling rack in it.

3 In a deep, straight-sided medium skillet, heat 2 inches (5 cm) of oil to 325°F (160°C). When the oil is hot, test the temperature by adding a small amount of panko to the hot oil — it should sizzle and brown up quickly when hot.

4 In a shallow bowl, beat the eggs. In a second shallow bowl, spread the panko in an even layer. Working with one piece of chicken at a time, tap off any excess marinade. Dip it into the egg and then cover it with panko. Set aside on a plate and repeat the dredging process with 3 to 5 more pieces of chicken.

5 Carefully distribute the pieces of breaded chicken in the hot oil and fry until golden brown on both sides, 3 to 4 minutes. While the chicken fries, bread a second batch of 4 to 6 pieces. Using a slotted spoon, transfer the cooked chicken to the prepared cooling rack, making sure none are touching. Allow the oil to come back up to temperature and fry the next batch of chicken. Repeat this process until all the chicken is cooked.

6 Serve warm or at room temperature and garnish with lemon wedges and the green parts of the scallion.

Mom's Crispy Pork Wontons

SKILL LEVEL: Moderate
PREP TIME: 40 minutes
COOK TIME: 30 minutes
YIELD: Makes 50 to 60 wontons

INGREDIENTS

FOR THE SWEET-AND-SOUR SAUCE

- ½ cup (120 ml) low-sodium chicken broth (store-bought is fine to use here)
- 2 tablespoons cornstarch
- ¾ cup (120 g) finely chopped pineapple; or a 6 ounce (170 g) can crushed pineapple, drained
- ½ cup (100 g) sugar
- ½ cup (120 g) ketchup
- ¼ cup (60 ml) rice vinegar

FOR THE WONTONS

- 8 ounces (220 g) ground pork
- 6–8 shrimp, about 8 ounces (220 g), shelled and deveined
- 1 large egg
- ½ cup (75 g) water chestnuts, drained
- 3 scallions, white and light green parts only
- 1 piece fresh ginger, about 1½ inches (3.5 cm), peeled
- 1 large fresh shiitake mushroom, stemmed
- 1 small garlic clove
- 1 tablespoon fresh parsley
- 1 teaspoon kosher salt
- ½ teaspoon freshly ground black pepper
- 1 package wonton wrappers, about 12 ounces (350 g), or round gyoza or potsticker wrappers
- Vegetable oil, for frying

My mom and her best friend, Tucky, used to make these wontons for our church's food festival, prepping thousands of them ahead of time and freezing them between layers of wax paper. I remember being in the church banquet hall filled with tables, and it seemed like the entire congregation was there to help. I'd sit with my brother, sister and cousins happily making wontons for hours. When wontons are defrosted, they can become soggy, so my mom and Tucky had a trick for their filling: instead of using regular onions (which weep when thawed), they used scallions. This recipe freezes well, so I highly recommend making the full batch of wontons even if you don't plan to eat them right away.

Also, the great part about this recipe is that these wontons can be either fried and served with a dipping sauce or simmered in a hot pot — it just comes down to how you assemble them. Fried wontons are folded to look like a boat with two sails and simmered wontons look like a cinched-up purse. The boat shape limits the filling to less meat, so the filling is able to cook through during the brief frying time; however, the cinched-up purse can hold more filling because the wontons can simmer for a longer time. If you want to try these in a soup, check out my Pork Wontons with Macanese Broth (page 77), where the wontons are cooked in a slightly sweet, aromatic pork-bone broth until perfectly tender.

1 Make the sweet-and-sour sauce. In a small saucepan, whisk together the chicken broth and cornstarch to make a slurry. Add the remaining sauce ingredients and whisk until smooth.

2 Place the saucepan over medium-low heat and bring the sauce to a simmer. Cook, whisking, until the sugar dissolves and the sauce is slightly thickened, about 10 minutes.

3 Make the wontons. In a food processor, combine the pork, shrimp, egg, water chestnuts, scallions, ginger, mushroom, garlic, parsley, salt and pepper. Pulse until well combined and a meatball-like texture is formed. If you do not have a food processor, finely chop the ingredients and mix to combine.

4 Assemble the wontons. Fill a small bowl with water and line a large airtight container with wax or parchment paper.

5 Working with 1 wonton wrapper at a time, place a rounded teaspoon of filling in the center of the wrapper. Be careful not to overstuff the wonton wrappers or they will be difficult to seal.

6 Wet your finger in the bowl of water and moisten the wrapper around the filling. Fold the bottom half of the wrapper up and away from you so the corners of the square are offset. Gently press the wonton wrapper together around the filling to seal. (If you are making these wontons for a hot pot, see Hot Tip.)

7 Transfer to the airtight container and repeat with the remaining filling and wonton wrappers, separating each layer of prepared wontons with wax or parchment paper.

8 Fill a large saucepan or a deep-fryer with 1½ inches (3.5 cm) of vegetable oil and heat over medium-high heat to 350°F (175°C). Line a rimmed baking sheet with paper towels. When the oil is hot, test the temperature by adding a small piece of wonton wrapper to the oil — it should fry up quickly when hot.

9 Working in small batches, carefully add the wontons to the hot oil. They should not be touching. Fry for about 5 minutes, until puffed, crispy and lightly browned. Using a slotted spoon, transfer the fried wontons to the paper towel–lined baking sheet to drain. Repeat with the remaining wontons.

10 Serve while hot with the sweet-and-sour sauce for dipping.

11 These wontons can be made ahead and frozen for up to 1 month. You can also refrigerate them overnight and fry them the next day, but don't refrigerate them for longer than that.

HOT TIP

If preparing these wontons to use in a hot pot, place 1 rounded tablespoon of filling in the center of a wonton square. Moisten the outside of the square with water and pinch up the opposite edges to make a square purse with sealed edges.

Korean Scallion Pancakes

SKILL LEVEL: Easy
PREP TIME: 20 minutes
COOK TIME: 20 minutes
YIELD: Makes 24 pancakes

INGREDIENTS

FOR THE BATTER

2 cups (240 g) cake flour
1 teaspoon baking powder
1 teaspoon kosher salt
½ teaspoon freshly ground black pepper
2 cups (480 ml) chilled club soda, plus more as needed
2 large eggs
1 tablespoon gochujang Korean chili paste
1 bunch scallions (approximately 10 stalks), thinly sliced on the bias
¼ cup (12 g) snipped fresh chives
¼ cup (40 g) toasted sesame seeds
Vegetable oil, for frying

FOR THE DIPPING SAUCE

¼ cup (60 ml) soy sauce
¼ cup (60 ml) rice vinegar
¼ cup (70 g) sweet chili sauce
2 teaspoons sesame oil

FOR THE GARNISH

Flaky sea salt
Fresh chive blossoms, optional

These Korean-style pancakes have a soft center and crunchy edges. The club soda reacts with the baking powder for a light and airy batter that translates to an ethereally crisp crust. I prefer to make smaller pancakes for a neat finger food and crispier edges.

1 To make the batter: In a medium bowl, whisk together the flour, baking powder, salt and pepper. In another medium bowl, whisk together the club soda, eggs and gochujang. Whisk the wet ingredients into the dry ingredients, being careful not to overmix. Chill for 15 minutes.

2 Make the dipping sauce by whisking together all the dipping sauce ingredients in a small bowl.

3 Preheat the oven to 200°F (90°C). Set a cooling rack on a rimmed baking sheet and place it on the middle rack of the oven. Remove the batter from the refrigerator and gently fold in the scallions, chives and sesame seeds. The pancake batter should have a thin consistency; if it's too thick, add more soda, ¼ cup (60 ml) at a time, and mix well until the consistency is thin.

4 Heat 2 tablespoons of vegetable oil in a medium skillet over medium-high heat. Add the batter in 2-tablespoon mounds and cook until crisp and golden brown, about 1 minute per side. Transfer to the rack in the oven to keep warm. Repeat with the remaining batter, adding vegetable oil to the pan for each batch.

5 To serve, sprinkle the pancakes with the flaky sea salt and chive blossoms, if using. Serve immediately with the dipping sauce.

HOT TIP

Cake flour is finer in texture and has a lower protein content (and therefore less gluten) than all-purpose flour, so when used it gives a more delicate texture and a better rise. If you want to make cake flour, use 1 cup (120 g) all-purpose flour minus 2 tablespoons, plus 2 tablespoons cornstarch. This will make 1 cup (120 g) cake flour.

Avocado with Sesame Seeds and Shoyu Koji

SKILL LEVEL: Moderate
PREP TIME: 10 minutes
YIELD: 4 to 6 servings

INGREDIENTS

¼ cup (60 ml) rice vinegar, or apple cider vinegar
¼ cup (60 ml) mirin
4 teaspoons shoyu koji
3 teaspoons sesame seeds, divided
¼ cup (60 ml) sesame oil
4 medium firm-ripe avocados, halved, pitted, peeled and cut into bite-size pieces
Optional garnishes: Crispy onions (such as Lars Own brand), furikake sprinkles, sesame seeds, fried garlic or sliced nori seaweed

Shoyu koji, also called soy sauce koji, is a savory condiment made of fermented rice and soy sauce. It adds instant umami to meat, fish, or vegetables in marinades or sauces, and is a more flavorful substitute for salt. This is one of my favorite sides because it's so addictive and versatile. Eat the marinated avocado on its own, toss in salads, or roll in a sheet of Roasted Nori Seaweed (page 39) with some steamed rice for a snack. Also, I garnish the salad with crispy onions and furikake, a Japanese spice mixture, but you could also sprinkle the avocado with thinly sliced roasted nori seaweed, sesame seeds or thinly sliced garlic crisped in some hot oil.

1 In a medium bowl, whisk together the vinegar, mirin, shoyu koji and 2 teaspoons of the sesame seeds.

2 While whisking, slowly drizzle in the sesame oil until incorporated.

3 Gently fold in the avocado.

4 Transfer to bowls and serve with the garnish of your choice.

Desserts

Coconut-Matcha Custard with Berries

SKILL LEVEL: Easy
PREP TIME: 30 minutes, plus 4 hours refrigeration time
YIELD: 8 servings

INGREDIENTS

2 cans full-fat coconut milk, 14 ounces (400 ml) each
2½ teaspoons gelatin, about one ¼-ounce (7 g) package
½ cup (170 g) maple syrup
1 teaspoon vanilla extract
2 teaspoons culinary-grade matcha powder
2 cups (250 g) fresh mixed berries, such as raspberries and blackberries
½ cup (40 g) toasted unsweetened shredded coconut
Small mint sprigs, for garnish

With so many foods chock-full of sugar, this dessert is truly good for the heart. It's gluten-free, has no refined sugar and is loaded with beneficial antioxidants from the matcha tea. Matcha in powdered form is available in Asian markets and online, and you will find a wide price range. For the purposes of this recipe, you don't have to buy it at a premium. The consistency of the custard is light and smooth; the berries give it a delicate tartness, and the crunch of the shredded coconut makes you want to keep digging in for more. This dessert is easy to make ahead of time — make the day before, then pull it out of the fridge when you're ready to serve. Just allow for the four hours the gelatin needs to set. Garnish with the berries, coconut and mint sprigs right before serving.

1   Arrange eight 8-ounce (240 ml) ramekins, small cups or glass bowls on a rimmed baking sheet.

2   In a small saucepan, whisk together the coconut milk and gelatin. Let sit for 5 minutes.

3   Whisk in the maple syrup, vanilla and matcha. Place the pan over medium-low heat and bring to a gentle simmer. Do not let the custard boil. Once the gelatin completely dissolves, remove from the heat.

4   Using a fine-mesh sieve, strain the custard into the ramekins, filling them about three-quarters full. Transfer the baking sheet to the refrigerator and let the custards cool until set, at least 4 hours.

5   To serve, top each custard with the berries and toasted coconut and garnish with the mint.

Emiko's Coffee Adzuki Jelly

SKILL LEVEL: Moderate
PREP TIME: 20 minutes, plus 5 to 6 hours refrigeration time
YIELD: Makes 48 squares

INGREDIENTS

Nonstick cooking spray, for preparing the pan

8 packets powdered gelatin, ¼ ounce (7 g) each

1¼ cups (300 ml) ice water

4½ cups (1 L) boiling water

¼ cup (60 ml) strong coffee, or 1 teaspoon instant coffee

2 cans sweetened condensed milk, 14 ounces (420 ml) each

1 can sweetened adzuki red beans, about 16 ounces (450 g)

In my family, we ring in the New Year with a big traditional Japanese feast, but I always leave room for this jelly dessert from my cousin Emiko. The sweet earthy adzuki beans settle to the bottom of the jelly which is then flipped before serving, making this an attractive bite after a big meal. The recipe makes a lot and the dessert is on the sweet side, so a small square per person is just enough.

1 Coat a 9 x 13-inch (23 x 33 cm) pan with cooking spray. Set aside.

2 In a large bowl, combine the gelatin and ice water. Let sit until softened, about 5 minutes.

3 Add the boiling water to the gelatin and stir until dissolved.

4 Stir in the coffee, sweetened condensed milk and adzuki beans. Pour the mixture into the prepared pan, giving it a little shake to make sure the mixture is evenly distributed. You want the beans to be evenly distributed throughout the bottom of the pan. Refrigerate until set, about 5 hours or overnight.

5 Cut the jelly into 1¼-inch (3 cm) rectangles, flip so the layer of beans is at the top of each piece, and serve.

Strawberry-Rose Mochi

SKILL LEVEL: Easy
PREP TIME: 5 minutes
COOK TIME: 10 minutes
YIELD: Makes 18 to 24 round patties

INGREDIENTS

¼ cup (16 g) small, dried, edible rosebuds (see Hot Tip)

¼ cup (40 g) katakuriko Japanese potato starch, or cornstarch

1 cup (160 g) mochi flour

1 cup (200 g) sugar

1 teaspoon strawberry-flavored gelatin, preferably organic

¼ teaspoon rose water

1 cup (240 ml) water

HOT TIP

It is important to have freshly dried rosebuds, as older ones can be less fragrant. Try to get your rosebuds from a quality tea provider if you can't find fresh ones online.

I love the sweet and floral combination of the strawberry gelatin and the crushed rose petals, but this recipe is easy to riff on. Try lime-flavored gelatin with some finely grated lime zest or mango gelatin with a dusting of chili powder — go wherever your imagination takes you.

My mom taught me it's essential to form mochi while the mochi paste is still piping hot. Because of this, I think I've burned off all my finger pads over the years. To avoid doing the same, I recommend kitchen gloves — this will make the mochi a little easier to handle. Although I don't normally use a microwave, it is the easiest and most efficient way of making this. If you don't have a microwave, you could also make this in a medium saucepan over medium heat. While working, you're looking for a soft and smooth consistency that is chewy and slightly sweet. Serve the mochi at the end of a meal or as a snack with a cup of hot green tea.

1 In a mini food processor or clean coffee grinder, pulse the rosebuds with the katakuriko until finely ground. Spread in a shallow bowl.

2 In a medium microwave-safe bowl, whisk together the mochi flour, sugar, gelatin, rose water and water until smooth. Cover with plastic wrap and microwave on high power for 3 minutes. Stir with a spatula, scraping down the sides. Microwave for 3 minutes more, or until thickened and all the liquid is absorbed.

3 Working in batches and wearing kitchen gloves, dip your fingers in the rose-katakuriko powder and pinch off a ping-pong–size ball of the hot mochi. Toss it in the rose-katakuriko powder, shaking off any excess. Holding the mochi in one hand, fold the edges of the mochi underneath itself using your other hand, while rotating it clockwise and forming a 1½- to 2-inch (3.5 to 5 cm) patty with a smooth top. Transfer to a plate and repeat with the remaining mochi.

4 Toss the cooled mochi with any remaining rose-katakuriko powder and serve.

5 The prepared mochi can be made ahead and refrigerated for up to 3 days, but they are best eaten on the day of preparation.

Chocolate Coconut Mochi Cake

SKILL LEVEL: Moderate
PREP TIME: 30 minutes
COOK TIME: 45 minutes
YIELD: 18 to 20 servings

INGREDIENTS

Nonstick cooking spray, for preparing the pan
2 cups (320 g) mochi flour
½ cup (60 g) cake flour (see Hot Tip)
½ cup (43 g) unprocessed cocoa powder
1 teaspoon baking soda
½ teaspoon kosher salt
2 cups (480 ml) whole milk
1 can coconut milk, 14 ounces (400 ml)
½ cup (140 g) melted dark, unsweetened chocolate, cooled slightly
1 teaspoon vanilla extract
5 large eggs, lightly beaten
1 stick salted butter, about 3½ oz (112 g), at room temperature
2 cups (400 g) packed dark brown sugar
Confectioners' sugar, for dusting
Ice cream, for serving

Mochi flour is a glutinous flour made from short-grain Japanese rice. The mochi flour in this cake gives it more density and moisture, while the cake flour and baking soda help it rise like a traditional cake. But, there's nothing traditional about it — the result is a rich, not-too-sweet, chocolatey confection that sticks to your fork and is somewhere between a brownie and a cake. My family prefers it heated a bit and served with a scoop of vanilla ice cream.

1 Preheat the oven to 350°F (175°C). Coat a 9 x 13-inch (23 x 33 cm) pan with cooking spray. Set aside.

2 In a medium bowl, whisk together the mochi flour, cake flour, cocoa powder, baking soda and salt.

3 In a separate medium bowl, whisk together the milk, coconut milk, melted chocolate, vanilla and eggs until smooth.

4 In the bowl of a stand mixer fitted with the paddle attachment, or in a large bowl and using a handheld electric mixer, cream the butter and brown sugar until light and fluffy, 3 to 4 minutes. Scrape down the sides.

5 With the mixer running, gradually add the dry and wet ingredients, alternating, until the batter is smooth and everything is just incorporated. Pour the batter into the prepared pan and smooth the top.

6 Bake for 40 to 45 minutes, until a toothpick inserted into the center comes out clean. Let cool in the pan for about 30 minutes.

7 Cut into thin slices and transfer to plates. Dust with the confectioners' sugar and serve with the ice cream.

HOT TIP

Cake flour is finer in texture and has a lower protein content (therefore less gluten) than all-purpose flour, so when used, it gives a more delicate texture and a better rise. If you want to make cake flour, use 1 cup (120 g) all-purpose flour minus 2 tablespoons, plus 2 tablespoons cornstarch, for 1 cup (120 g) cake flour.

Yuzu Citrus Sorbet

SKILL LEVEL: Moderate
PREP TIME: 35 minutes, plus 4 hours freezing time
YIELD: 8 servings

INGREDIENTS

4 cups (800 g) sugar
4 cups (940 ml) water
1 cup (240 ml) yuzu juice (from 8 fresh small yuzu or from a bottle), or the juice of 4 small lemons and 4 small limes
1½ tablespoons freshly grated orange zest
Fresh mint leaves, for garnish

When I was younger, my mom used to throw these fabulous dinner parties with her friends, complete with the finest china, silver and beautiful printed menus. The women who threw these elaborate suppers called themselves The Dames. I remember one evening when my mom let me have a taste of a lemon sorbet that they were serving in cutout lemon baskets — I'll never forget it. This sorbet is my tribute to The Dames. Here, I use tart yuzu citrus instead of lemon. While I might not serve this in a hand-carved citrus basket, I still think they would approve.

1 Make an ice bath by filling a large aluminum or glass bowl halfway with ice and then covering the ice with cold water until the bowl is three-quarters full.

2 In a medium saucepan over medium-high heat, whisk together the sugar and water. Bring to a boil. Cook for about 5 minutes, whisking, until the sugar dissolves and a syrup is formed. Carefully pour the hot syrup into a medium bowl and set the bowl in the ice bath to cool, whisking every 5 minutes until completely cooled, about 20 minutes in all.

3 Remove the bowl from the ice bath and stir in the yuzu juice and orange zest to form the sorbet base. Pour the sorbet base into a 9 x 13-inch (23 x 33 cm) baking dish and transfer to the freezer. Freeze the sorbet, stirring the mixture every hour with a fork, until set, soft and smooth, at least 4 hours.

4 Scoop the sorbet into small bowls, garnish with the mint leaves and serve right away.

Index

Photo Credits

Published by Tuttle Publishing, an imprint of
Periplus Editions (HK) Ltd.

www.tuttlepublishing.com

ISBN: 978-4-8053-1719-8

Distributed by
North America, Latin America & Europe
Tuttle Publishing
364 Innovation Drive
North Clarendon, VT 05759-9436 U.S.A.
Tel: 1 (802) 773-8930
Fax: 1 (802) 773-6993
info@tuttlepublishing.com
www.tuttlepublishing.com

Japan
Tuttle Publishing
Yaekari Building 3rd Floor
5-4-12 Osaki
Shinagawa-ku
Tokyo 141-0032
Tel: (81) 3 5437-0171
Fax: (81) 3 5437-0755
sales@tuttle.co.jp
www.tuttle.co.jp

Asia Pacific
Berkeley Books Pte. Ltd.
3 Kallang Sector #04-01
Singapore 349278
Tel: (65) 6741 2178
Fax: (65) 6741 2179
inquiries@periplus.com.sg
www.tuttlepublishing.com

25 24 23 22
10 9 8 7 6 5 4 3 2 1

Printed in China   2210EP

"Books to Span the East and West"

Tuttle Publishing was founded in 1832 in the small New England town of Rutland, Vermont [USA]. Our
core values remain as strong today as they were then — to publish best-in-class books which bring people together one page at a time. In 1948, we established a publishing office in Japan — and Tuttle is now a
leader in publishing English-language books about the arts, languages and cultures of Asia. The world has
become a much smaller place today and Asia's economic and cultural influence has grown. Yet the need for
meaningful dialogue and information about this diverse region has never been greater. Over the past seven
decades, Tuttle has published thousands of books on subjects ranging from martial arts and paper crafts to
language learning and literature — and our talented authors, illustrators, designers and photographers have
won many prestigious awards. We welcome you to explore the wealth of information available on Asia at
www.tuttlepublishing.com.